Advance Praise for

The Nurse's Etiquette Advantage

"With her background as a nurse, educator, consultant, and professional speaker, Kathleen D. Pagana provides practical advice that will take you from your first nursing position to the boardroom. This straightforward, easy-to-read guide is interesting, informative, and helpful in both business and social settings. *The Nurse's Etiquette Advantage* addresses modern realities such as smoking, technology, and body piercings and provides fresh guidelines on etiquette from a nursing perspective. You can feel reassured that you are behaving the correct way when you arm yourself with the wisdom and knowledge found in *The Nurse's Etiquette Advantage*."

—Peg Gray-Vickrey, DNS, RN, Interim Provost,
Vice President of Academic Affairs, and Professor of Nursing
Florida Gulf Coast University

"This book takes what could be a dull subject and makes it fun! Readers will be amazed at how much they didn't know and how this book, which specifically targets nurses, provides many useful lessons that will be the secret ingredient for future career successes."

—Karlene Kerfoot, PhD, RN, CNNA, FAAN
Vice President/Chief Clinical Officer
Aurora Health Care
Milwaukee, WI

"*The Nurse's Etiquette Advantage* is a must-read for nursing students who want to advance their career with finesse and grace. It is a good reminder that 'you never get a second chance to make a first impression!'"

—Diane J. Mancino, EdD, RN, CAE
Executive Director
National Student Nurses' Association and the
Foundation of the NSNA

"*The Nurse's Etiquette Advantage* is a must-read for all nurses who want to boost their confidence and credibility and avoid embarrassment in their personal and professional life. The advice offered is the perfect complement to clinical education and experience. It will assist any nurse in developing into a well-rounded, socially adept professional."

—Donna Cardillo, MA, RN
Nursing Career Guru
Dear Donna columnist for *Nursing Spectrum/NurseWeek*

The Nurse's Etiquette Advantage

How Professional Etiquette Can Advance
Your Nursing Career

By Kathleen D. Pagana, PhD, RN

Sigma Theta Tau International
Honor Society of Nursing®

Sigma Theta Tau International

Editor-in-Chief: Jeff Burnham
Acquisitions Editor: Cynthia Saver, RN, MS
Project Editor: Carla Hall
Copy Editor and Indexer: Jane Palmer
References: Melody Jones

Cover Design: Gary Adair
Interior Design and Page Composition: Rebecca Harmon
Illustrator: Amanda Emig

Printed in the United States of America
Printing and Binding by Printing Partners, Indianapolis, IN

Sigma Theta Tau International
550 West North Street
Indianapolis, IN 46202

Visit our Web site at **www.nursingsociety.org** for more information on our books.
ISBN-10: 1-930538-80-4
ISBN-13: 978-1-930538-80-1

Library of Congress Cataloging-in-Publication Data

Pagana, Kathleen Deska, 1952-
  The nurse's etiquette advantage : how professional etiquette can advance your nursing career / by Kathleen D. Pagana.
     p. ; cm.
  Includes bibliographical references and index.
  ISBN 978-1-930538-80-1
  1. Nursing—Social aspects. 2. Business etiquette. I. Sigma Theta Tau International. II. Title.
  [DNLM: 1. Nurses—psychology. 2. Career Mobility. 3. Interprofessional Relations. 4. Professional Competence. WY 87 P128n 2008]
  RT86.5.P34 2008
  362.17'3—dc22
                                        2008016402

07 08 09 10 11 / 5 4 3 2 1

Dedication

This book is dedicated with love, admiration, and gratitude to my husband, Timothy J. Pagana.

Acknowledgements

This book would not have been possible without help, support, or inspiration from so many people. I want to express my special thanks to the following people:

Rosalinda Alfaro-LeFevre

Marjorie Brody

Lynne Breil

Donna Cardillo

Marianne P. Deska

Sandy Dumont

Amanda Emig

Kathleen O. Engelmeier

Jocelyn P. Gaul

Amy Glass

Carla Hall

Becky Harmon

Carol M. Headley

Vicki Hess

James S. Huggins

Diane Langley

Joan Massella

Nicole Nardi

Denise K. Pagana

Theresa N. Pagana

Timothy J. Pagana

Jane Palmer

Cynthia Saver

Juanell Teague

A. Kay Tyberg

Table of Contents

Introduction

Nursing education focuses on leadership, management, and professional issues, while etiquette is the "missing link" for success in the workplace.

This book describes how to get a job, keep a job, and move ahead in a job. It will prepare you to handle awkward and challenging situations that could diminish your confidence, tarnish your reputation, and derail your career aspirations. After reading this enjoyable book, you will be able to interact more effectively in clinical, business, and social settings. You will be amazed at how often you will think, "I didn't know how much I needed to know."

The premise is that anyone can become an expert in etiquette. Further, the more skilled you become, the more you will be offered opportunities and positions. In these pages, you will find a "reality check" for those playing (or about to play) the toughest sport of all—survival in a business world that is often unforgiving and highly critical.

Why is etiquette important for nurses? Etiquette is about relationships. Nursing is a career characterized by professional relationships with all kinds of people in all kinds of settings. By using the guiding principles of kindness, consideration, and common sense, professional etiquette can help you initiate new relationships and enhance established relationships. It can guide you in unfamiliar situations and help you know what to expect from others. For example, this book can help you in the following situations:

* Interviewing successfully for a new job or position

* Introducing yourself and others with confidence

* Demonstrating proper handshake and business-card etiquette

* Networking effectively on the job and at conferences

* Dressing to mirror your professional image and responsibilities

* Sending a positive impression with thank-you notes and letters

* Using e-mail, phone, and fax in a courteous and professional manner

* Dining with confidence in any business or social setting

* Increasing your comfort and self-confidence during business travel

* Appreciating and respecting cultural difference in global inter-actions

There are no other etiquette books targeted and customized to nurses. This book contains key business-etiquette content with an application to professional nursing. It will help you "level the playing field" in your interactions with others.

Key Features

Each chapter challenges the reader with *Do you know* ... questions.

Do you:

Know what to do when you meet a colleague whose name you have forgotten?

Know how to introduce your spouse to your boss?

Know what to do if your client ignores your attempt to shake hands?

Have trouble remembering names?

Wonder when it is appropriate to give out your business card?

A unique feature of this book is its organization in a "question and answer" format. This allows you to target what you need or want to learn or review.

(2) **Is there anything that can be done about sweaty hands?**

Yes, spray them with an antiperspirant once a day. This usually takes about 24 hours to become effective. It that does not work, see your physician.

What is a two-handed handshake?

In this situation, the right hand shakes your right hand, but the person's left hand is placed on your body. The most common left-handed positions are on the wrist, forearm, biceps, shoulder, or neck.

(3)

Tips highlight important points for you to remember.

TIP

Never approach someone and say, "Do you remember me?" Be considerate. Put out your hand and state your name.

(4)

Faux Pas and *Good Idea!* boxes provide stories that model embarrassing and positive actions.

 ✗ *Faux Pas*

 ✓ *Good Idea!*

Tables and figures help itemize and illustrate concrete information.

1.1 Pecking Order for Introductions

Higher Ranking	Lower Ranking
VP of nursing	New nurse
10-year employee	2-year employee
Father	Daughter's boyfriend
Your boss	Your spouse
Peer in another office	Peer in your office
Client	Colleague

 Cultural items are marked with a globe.

Helpful frequently asked questions (FAQs) are included in each chapter.

 ## Frequently Asked Questions

 What if I am introducing my boss to my new staff member and I mention the staff member's name first?

Just continue with the introduction and try to remember the proper pecking order the next time. The most important thing about introductions is to make them.

Each chapter ends with
"Take-Away Tips."

TAKE-AWAY TIPS

✓ **Make an effort to remember names
when meeting people.**

✓ **People are judged by the quality of
their handshake.**

Finally . . .

"I never knew etiquette could be so much fun," is the most common
response to people encountering professional etiquette presentations
for the first time. The goal of this book is for you to learn (or recall)
some career-enhancing material and to have fun at the same time.

Basically, you have nothing to lose and everything to gain by reading
this book. The skills you learn can be put into practice immediately
for career advancement and lifelong value.

Professional etiquette is not optional for personal or professional
success—it is a necessity. You can benefit every day in clinical, business, and social settings by using *The Nurse's Etiquette Advantage*
to come across as polished, confident, and professional.

Business Etiquette

Test Your Knowledge

1. Where would you find your salad plate?

   To the right of the entrée plate.   To the left of the entrée plate.

2. You can demonstrate professional use of e-mail by including a greeting and a close.

   True   False

3. It is more professional for a woman to wear a suit with a skirt than a suit with pants.

   True   False

4. It doesn't matter how much jewelry a woman wears to a job interview.

   True   False

5. Sending a thank-you note by e-mail is perfectly acceptable.

   True   False

6. If you don't have a business card, it's OK to ask for someone's card and write your contact information on the back.

   True   False

7. A business meal is a time to relax and "let loose."

   True   False

8. Whose name do you say first when introducing your new nurse manager to your VP of nursing?

    Nurse manager   VP of nursing

9. People sitting on the train next to you think you are important if you are talking on your cell phone.

    True   False

10. When making a phone call, always be prepared to leave a voice-mail message.

    True   False

11. What do you do if your name is mispronounced when you are introduced?

    Repeat your name correctly   Ignore the error

12. It is appropriate to tell an associate that she has spinach in her teeth.

    True   False

13. A man should wait for a woman in business to extend her hand for a handshake.

    True   False

14. It doesn't matter how you dress for your position, because "people don't judge a book by its cover."

    True   False

15. If you need to excuse yourself during a meal, where do you place your napkin?

16. When holding a drink at a cocktail party, hold it in your left hand.

True   False

17. When traveling abroad for business, you should be prepared with a working knowledge of appropriate global etiquette.

True   False

18. While checking in at a conference, you are given a name badge holder. You should insert your business card into the holder.

True   False

19. Name two topics to avoid discussing at a business cocktail party.

20. It is OK to smoke before an interview.

True   False

1

Making Your Acquaintance

Introductions

These are concerns that can add to the stress of any situation where you are meeting and greeting new people. Who hasn't felt awkward during some introductions? You will feel and act more confident if you understand the basic guidelines, and you can improve your interactions with others by practicing these tips for making introductions and creating a positive first impression.

"Civility costs nothing and buys everything."
—Lady Mary Wortley Montagu

Introductions

Does it really matter who is introduced to whom in an introduction?

Yes, it does. There is a pecking order to introductions. The person of honor is mentioned first, and the other person is introduced to him or her. The person of honor is the higher-ranking person in the organization. For example, suppose a new graduate is being introduced to the vice president of nursing. The vice president of nursing is mentioned first, and the new nurse is presented or introduced to him or her.

What are the key steps of an introduction?

Introductions should have three steps.

1. Mention the name of the person of honor first.

2. Say the name of the person being introduced and mention something about him or her.

3. Come back to the person of honor and say something about him or her.

Here is an example of a proper introduction following the three steps above.

> "Theresa, I would like to present Walt Deska. Walt is our new staff nurse with 3 years' experience in orthopedics. Theresa Williams has been our VP of nursing for the past 5 years."

Here is a way to facilitate conversation after an introduction, using the example above.

> "Theresa, I would like to present Walt Deska. Walt is our new staff nurse with 3 years' experience in orthopedics. He is also a marathon runner. Theresa has been our VP of nursing for the past 5 years. She is training for her first marathon."

(1.1) Pecking Order for Introductions

Higher Ranking	Lower Ranking
VP of nursing	New nurse
10-year employee	2-year employee
Father	Daughter's boyfriend
Your boss	Your spouse
Peer in another office	Peer in your office
Client	Colleague

When should I introduce myself?

Always be ready to introduce yourself. None of us is a famous movie star with face and name recognition. Don't stand next to someone, waiting to be introduced. The person you are expecting to introduce you may have forgotten your name. So, to prevent embarrassing him or her, just introduce yourself. Put out your hand and say your name. For example, "I don't believe we've met. I'm Denise Miller." Or, "Hello, I'm Denise Miller, and I am a nurse in Same Day Surgery." The other person should return your greeting and introduce himself or herself. If he or she does not give a name, say, "And your name is _____?"

TIP Never approach someone and say, "Do you remember me?" Be considerate. Put out your hand and state your name.

What should I do if I go blank and cannot remember someone's name when making an introduction?

This happens. Be honest about it. You can say, "I'm sorry, but I've forgotten your name." Or, "Excuse me, but I'm blanking on your name."

Handshaking

Are you judged by the quality of your handshake?

Yes, you are. You want to present a confident and firm handshake. Those few seconds you "shake" can weaken or empower a relationship. The handshake is part of creating a first impression and sending a parting message. Follow these three steps for a proper handshake.

1. Extend your right hand horizontally with your thumb up. (Do not cup your hand.)

2. Engage a person's hand web-to-web with a firm grip. (The web between your thumb and index finger should be touching the other person's thumb web.)

3. Shake two or three times and drop your hand.

1.2 Handshake Etiquette

DO	DON'T
Stand up	Remain seated
Make eye contact	Shake with limp, damp fingers
Offer a firm grip	Squeeze the hand too tightly
Smile	Turn the person's hand over
Be considerate of personal space issues	Refuse to shake hands

"A firm, hearty handshake gives a good first impression, and you'll never be forgotten if you don't live up to it."

—P.J. O'Rourke

Is there anything that can be done about sweaty hands?

Yes, spray them with an antiperspirant once a day. This usually takes about 24 hours to become effective. It that does not work, see your physician.

What is a two-handed handshake?

In this situation, the right hand shakes your right hand, but the person's left hand is placed on your body. The most common left-handed positions are on the wrist, forearm, biceps, shoulder, or neck. The higher the left hand moves up the body, the greater the possibility for manipulation and control. For example, a left hand clasped around the neck may imply intimacy or ownership (Brown & Johnson, 2004). Coming from someone you have just met, the two-handed handshake should alert you to the possibility of a controlling situation or manipulation. However, this may be perfectly acceptable for friendly, long-term colleagues.

Handshake Variations and Possible Implications

HANDSHAKE	POSSIBLE INTERPRETATION
Dead fish *(cold and clammy)*	Passive personality with low self-esteem
Pull-in *(holds onto your hand and moves you)*	Person is maneuvering you and wants to place you somewhere.
Hand on top *(dominant person has palm facing down in relation to the other)*	Person wants to be in control
Finger squeeze	Wants to keep other person at a comfortable distance
Twister *(grabs your hand and twists it under his or hers)*	Wants you in a submissive position
Bone crusher *(extreme finger squeezer)*	Person equates brute strength with power

(Brown & Johnson, 2004)

Does gender play a role in handshaking?

In the United States, business is gender-neutral. A man or a woman may initiate the handshake. However, at social gatherings, it is often considered prudent for a man to wait for a woman, especially an elderly woman, to offer her hand.

What should I do if someone ignores my attempt to shake hands?

Gently drop your hand back to your side. There are many cultural preferences and sensitivities that impact a handshake. For example, in the Hindu culture, contact between men and women is avoided, and men do not shake hands with women. There also may be physical limitations or sickness issues.

 ### Does handshake etiquette differ in other countries?

Yes. If you are traveling to other parts of the world, do some research before leaving home. For example, in Germany, a man should wait for a businesswoman to extend her hand for the handshake.

Remembering Names

How can I remember names?

Here are some tips for remembering names:

* Listen carefully. Often, we are more interested in impressing others than listening to and focusing on others.

* Repeat the person's name. For example, "It is a pleasure to meet you, Arlene."

* Try to connect the person's name to someone. For example, "Margaret, that is also my mother's name and my middle name."

* Try to connect the name to something. For example, Rose has red hair like my rose bushes.

* Ask the person to spell or repeat his or her name. For example, "Do you spell Katharine with a 'C' or a 'K'?"

* Look at the person's name tag during the introduction.

* Write down the name or ask for a business card. This will help you remember names for the long run.

* Ask the person for a helpful way to remember how to pronounce his or her name. For example, when people ask me how to pronounce "Pagana," I tell them to think of the word "banana." Then say, "Pah-gann-a" like "bah-nann-a."

* Try using the acronym CAR to help you remember names.

    * Concentrate on hearing and remembering the name.

    * Associate the name with something or someone.

    * Repeat the name in your conversation.

What if I met someone before and forgot his or her name?

Say something like: "I met you before. I am not good with names. My name is _____." The other person should say his or her name.

If someone mispronounces my name, should I grin and bear it?

No. It is a kindness to correct the person right away in a casual and friendly manner. The delay may add to his or her embarrassment.

X Faux Pas

Dorothy frequently called the medical office of Dr. Nguyen. She pronounced the name "Nu-gen" with a long "U." Several weeks later, she learned from a colleague that the correct pronunciation of the doctor's name was "When." She called the office to apologize and was told that the staff had been getting a good laugh out of this mispronunciation for weeks.

Business Cards

Do I need a business card?

Yes, you do. Business cards are a great way to capture essential information in a quick and user-friendly manner. Every professional needs a business card for networking. Patients love having business cards from their health care providers because it gives them important contact information. Business cards can be attached with any report or note you are sending. This lets the person know that you are the sender and provides your contact information.

What information should be on my business card?

That will depend on the purpose of the card. Some basics include your name, credentials, position, and contact information, including address, phone, e-mail address, and fax number. If your name is ambiguous (such as "Pat" or "Terry"), use your full name ("Patricia"/"Patrick" or "Teresa"/"Terrance") if applicable, or add a title (for example, Mr. or Ms. Pat Smith). If you are trying to promote a service, such as writing consultant, make sure that is included on your card. Include your Web site if you have one.

Do you have any recommendations about the confusing alphabet soup that many nurses use after their names for their academic and certification credentials?

According to Smolenski (2002), this alphabet soup approach can be confusing to the public, other health care providers, and nurses themselves. There are basically six types of credentials that can be used after a name:

1. Degree (for example, BSN, MSN, PhD, DNS, EdD)

2. Licensure (for example, RN, LPN)

X *Faux Pas*

Mike was eating lunch at a national nursing convention. At the end of the meal, a new colleague asked him for his business card. Mike took his wallet from his back pocket and pulled out a warm, mushy business card. He quickly learned that his cards were not stored in a professional manner.

✓ *Good Idea!*

Recently a colleague asked me if I wanted to run with her in a race to support a cardiac center. When I asked for details, she wrote the Web site address on the back of her business card and asked me to call her with any questions. Isn't that better than writing on a table napkin?

3. State designation or entitlement (for example, APN, CRNP)

4. National certification (for example, RN, C)

5. Awards of honor (for example, Fellow of the American Academy of Nursing [FAAN])

6. Other certifications (for example, certification for computer skills)

For individuals with multiple credentials, Smolenski (2002) recommends the general rule of following the name with the highest credential that can least be taken away from you, in descending order, with awards or fellowships last. For example, let's use Janet Swingler, PhD, RN, APRN, as an example. The PhD degree cannot be taken away. The licensure could be revoked and the certification could be taken away if the licensure is lost. Janet could certainly list additional degrees and credentials if it would help her when applying for a particular position. However, usually only the highest degree is used. It is not necessary to use PhD, MSN, and BSN.

Is it OK to make my own business cards?

Only if that is the only way you will get a card. Homemade cards look homemade. There are Web sites that offer free cards for a minor shipping charge. Keep in mind that a business card is one of the first graphic impressions of you and your services.

How should I carry my business cards?

It is best to use a business-card holder or something else that will keep the cards in good condition. A cheap solution is to use a plastic name-tag holder.

Make sure the card you give is in good condition. Don't use a card if it is soiled, bent, or ripped, because the card will not reflect a positive impression of you. *It is better to give no card than to give one that is in bad condition.*

Develop a system for handling your business cards. For example, keep the cards you give out in your right pocket and place the ones you receive in your left pocket. This will prevent accidentally handing out someone else's card.

> **TIP**
>
> **The business card is often described as the handshake you leave behind. Make sure you leave a good impression.**

Is there a proper way to pass out a business card?

Yes, cards should be presented with the content face up and readable. The receiver should be able to glance at the card and make a comment. For example, "I see you're the clinical nurse specialist in the ICU."

What are some common mistakes that people make with business cards?

* Passing out your cards as if you are dealing a deck of cards. (You want to be asked for your card. To achieve this, ask for the other

person's card first. He or she will most likely ask for yours in return.)

* Writing on someone's card without asking permission. In some parts of the world, such as Japan, the business card is viewed as a representation of the owner. You deface the card if you write on it without permission.

* Not having your cards with you. You never know when someone will ask for your card. Keep them with you at all times. A business-card holder will keep your cards looking professional.

* Not having a card and asking for someone else's card to write on the back. This is rude. Jot your information on a piece of paper and make sure this doesn't happen again.

Karen was relaxing in the hotel lobby after attending a conference in Los Angeles. She met another nurse, Betty, who was in the process of setting up an ambulatory surgery center. Betty asked Karen for a business card. Karen did not have her cards with her, so she asked for one of Betty's cards, crossed out Betty's information, and wrote her contact information on the back of the card. Karen did not even realize that this was rude.

 Does business-card etiquette differ around the world?

Yes. If you will be traveling in a foreign country for business, do some research on business-card etiquette before leaving home. People in some countries, such as Germany, are impressed by education and like to see all degrees and titles above the bachelor's degree. In Saudi Arabia, the card should be printed in English on one side and Arabic on the other. When traveling to Poland, bring plenty of cards and give one to everyone you meet.

✓ *Good Idea!*

Recently a new family moved into our neighborhood. As they
met the neighbors, they gave everyone a business card with their
names (parents and children), address, and phone number. What
an impressive way to meet new neighbors and be remembered!

Frequently Asked Questions

 **What if I am introducing my boss to my new staff
member and I mention the staff member's name
first?**

Just continue with the introduction and try to remember the
proper pecking order the next time. The most important thing
about introductions is to make them.

 **What should I say about myself when I introduce
myself?**

This depends on the situation. If it is work-related, mention
your position in the organization. If it is a social situation,
mention something pertinent to the setting. For example, if
you are at a neighborhood party at Mike's house, you might
say: "My name is Ella Gaul. Mike is my next-door neighbor."

 **I have heard that it is a good idea to be the last one
to release your hand from a handshake. What do
you think?**

Some experts consider the pause at the end of a handshake
a key ingredient of a successful handshake. Pausing demonstrates confidence and expresses sincerity and openness.

What are my options if I am being introduced to someone and they sneeze into their right hand and then extend their hand for a handshake?

You can shake their hand and then go to the restroom and wash your hands. People often refer to this as "taking one for the team." Or, you can say you are getting over a cold and would prefer not to shake hands.

 What do you think of having more than one business card?

This is a great idea if it will help you target your business to a specific audience. For example, if you are a part-time freelance writer, it would be great to have a card related to that and separate from your main job.

 Is it OK to use up your supply of business cards if some of your contact information has changed?

Only use them as a temporary measure while you are waiting for your updated ones. Then, throw away the outdated cards. Next time, arrange to get new cards before your information changes.

 Should a man wait for a businesswoman to extend her hand first for the handshake?

Not anymore. Because American business is gender-neutral, this is no longer the case. However, in a social setting, a man often will wait for a woman to extend her hand first. Handshaking etiquette is different in other cultures.

 Is there any way to personalize your business cards?

Yes, business cards can benefit from the personal touch. For example, you may add your cell phone number on the back if you are hard to reach when traveling. It is a thoughtful gesture that will be appreciated.

What do you do with the business cards you collect after an event?

On the back of the card, note where you met the person and any pertinent information that you want to remember. Add the date.

 I recently graduated after a long climb up the ladder. As a result, I have obtained many degrees and licenses (LPN, RN, AA, AS, BSN, MSN). What should I include after my name?

Put your highest degree and your professional licensure after your name. The highest degree assumes the prerequisite degrees. For example, I would use "Deborah Tooney, MSN, RN." If you are speaking to a group of LPNs, you could add the LPN to connect with the audience.

 What should I do if someone does not have a business card, and I would like to have his or her contact information?

Take one of your business cards and cross out your information on the front. This will prevent you from accidentally giving this card to someone else. Then write his or her contact information on the back.

 What can I do if I forget the name of someone I need to introduce to another person?

Here are two suggestions for handling this situation: First, introduce the person you already know. For example, "I'd like you to meet Donald Smith." This will usually result in the third person introducing himself or herself. Second, you can say, "I'm sorry, but I've forgotten your name." Then, make the introductions.

TAKE-AWAY TIPS

✓ **Make an effort to remember names when meeting people.**

✓ **People are judged by the quality of their handshake.**

✓ **The handshake is the only socially acceptable form of touch that can be used in a business situation with a person of the same or opposite sex without raising eyebrows.**

✓ **The business card is sometimes described as "the handshake you leave behind."**

✓ **The most important thing to remember about introductions is to make them.**

✓ **Ask for the other person's business card, and he or she will usually ask for yours.**

✓ **Present your business card with the content face up and readable to the recipient.**

✓ **The person who receives a business card should look at it and make a comment.**

2

When Talk's Not Cheap

Conversations and Networking for Career Success

Do you:

Know how to start a conversation during a networking opportunity?

Need to improve your listening skills?

Wonder if a certain topic is safe to bring up?

Know the proper placement of a name tag?

Know how to gracefully exit a conversation when it is time to move on?

These are concerns that most people have in networking situations. Unfortunately, with the emphasis today on electronic communication, some of our interpersonal skills have been neglected. This has weakened our confidence and skill in face-to-face communication. As an example, think of going to a gym. Note the number of people with earphones plugged in. They do not even say "hello" to others.

The ability to connect with colleagues, clients, and co-workers is essential for success. Read on for some tips designed to make you more confident and professional at work and in social situations.

Conversational Topics

What topics are safe for conversation?

When you are making new acquaintances within a professional setting, it is best to avoid controversial topics. See Table 2.1 for a list of safe and taboo conversational topics.

2.1 Conversational Topics	
SAFE	**UNSAFE**
Weather	Politics
Sports	Religion
Traffic	Salary or cost of items
Travel	Jokes of questionable taste
Movies and books	Medical problems
Current events	Gossip
Olympics	Personal misfortunes
New developments in science	Controversial issues

Is it OK to talk about children?

Yes. If people ask about your children, answer briefly. Be careful of monopolizing the conversation talking about all the great things your children are doing. Be sensitive to the fact that some people may not be able to have children. People without children may also be bored hearing about your children.

"Your listeners won't care how much you know until they know how much you care."
—Anonymous

What are some attributes of a good conversationalist?

In addition to being polite and truly caring about others, here is a helpful list.

* Shows interest in others.

* Keeps abreast of major news items.

* Makes good eye contact when speaking.

* Pays attention to body language.

* Doesn't pre-judge others.

* Avoids correcting a person's grammar in public.

* Accepts compliments gracefully.

* Knows how to pay a compliment.

* Addresses everyone in the group.

* Does not monopolize the conversation.

* Knows how to make a shy person feel included.

* Knows how to ask questions without prying.

* Steps in to fill an embarrassing void in the conversation.

X *Faux Pas*

Marlene was interviewing for a faculty position. Janet was taking her through the library as part of her tour around the campus. Marlene made no comments and did not ask any questions throughout the tour. Her responses were all one-word replies. When the dean met with Marlene, the 45-minute scheduled interview was completed in 15 minutes. All of Marlene's evaluations were negative, and she was not offered the position.

The Art of Small Talk

Is small talk really important?

Yes. Small talk is an easy way to start conversations until you find a common area of interest or until business begins. It is used to break the ice and make people feel comfortable. It is a gateway to new relationships and is also important for maintaining established relationships. The bottom line is this: *There is nothing small about small talk.*

"One always speaks badly when one has nothing to say."

—Voltaire

Do you have any tips for breaking the ice with small talk?

Yes, try using the acronym OAR to aid your conversation.

* **O**bserve. Make an observation. (For example, "It looks like there are 500 people here.")

* **A**sk questions. (For example, "Is this your first time in San Diego?")

* **R**eveal something about yourself. (For example, "This is my fifth time attending the convention.")

It is a great idea to practice this technique. You can do this anytime and anywhere. For example, you can be standing in the cafeteria line with a colleague, waiting for a meeting to begin, or chatting with the grocery store clerk at checkout.

Networking

How important is networking for career development?

Networking is about forming relationships. It is essential for career development because these relationships can benefit you, the other person, your careers, and your life. These relationships connect you with new colleagues and with new opportunities, new information, and different professional practice settings. Think of networking as part of your career, not an add-on if you have time (Pachter, 2006b).

How can you prepare for a networking session at a conference?

Prepare by being well-read. Read newspapers, magazines, and key journals related to your conference or specialty. Find out who is going to be there, and plan to meet at least several new people. Networking is a powerful way to make new contacts and form new professional and personal contacts.

What is the key for "working the room" at a business or social event?

The key is to demonstrate respect, courtesy, and consideration for the feelings of others as you stay alert for networking opportunities. Good manners are good for business, and bad manners may mean no business. We may forget what people say to us, but we remember how they made us feel.

Working the room does not entail flitting from person to person, handing out your business cards, and pumping hands with as many people as possible in a short period of time. If you don't care about people, they will easily sense your insincerity.

> **TIP**
>
> **If you can spot someone "working a room," they are doing it wrong.**

How do you recommend working the room?

The easiest person to approach is the single person standing alone. That person will appreciate your walking up and introducing yourself.

Closed Stance   Open Stance

If you see couples, take note if they are in an open or closed position. If they are in the open stance (standing side by side), feel free to approach and introduce yourself. If they are in the closed stance (standing face to face), this implies that they are having a private conversation. Don't approach them.

With groups of three, note the open or closed standing positions. Approach the group with the open stance. If you observe a large group of four or more people standing in a circle, that group is closed.

As you can see, there are basically six ways that people assemble at a networking event:

1. Standing alone
2. The open two
3. The open three
4. The closed two
5. The closed three
6. Larger groups standing in a circle

The first three types of groups will generally be welcoming. Avoid the latter three unless you know someone in the group (Kintish, 2006).

What should I say as I approach a person or group that I do not know?

Smile and say, "Hello, may I join you?" Then, introduce yourself and use small talk to get acquainted.

What can I do if I hear myself talking too much?

You do not want to monopolize the conversation. You can demonstrate your interest in others by letting them speak.

TIP

Even when you are a guest at an event, act like a host. When you think like a host, you act in a different way. You will be more confident, purposeful, and certain.

Remember the old adage that you were given two ears and one mouth for a reason. You want to listen more than you speak. Here are two acronyms to keep you on track (Kintish, 2006).

WAIT: **W**hy **A**m **I** **T**alking?

STALL: **S**top **T**alking **A**nd **L**isten & **L**earn

2.2 Common Networking Mistakes and How to Avoid Them

Networking mistakes	Tips to avoid mistakes
Skipping the networking reception at a conference	Arrive early to mingle with other guests or the speaker
Approaching the event with a negative attitude	Approach the event with enthusiasm
Focusing on your personal agenda	Try to be a resource for others
Forgetting your business cards	Always carry your business cards with you
Not writing down pertinent information	Jot down notes on the back of a business card
Connecting only with your friends	Expand your network by making some new contacts
Not following up afterward	Schedule time afterward for follow-up

What is the best way to handle a compliment?

Smile and graciously say, "Thank you." Here are some helpful hints for giving or receiving a compliment:

∗ Refusing a compliment makes you look unprofessional.

* Don't feel compelled to return the compliment.

* Do not ask where someone bought his or her outfit or how much it cost.

* Do not brag about your designer labels.

* Make sure you are sincere when complimenting someone (Mitchell, 2000).

What is the proper placement for a name tag?

The name tag should be placed on the right side of the chest so it can be easily seen when shaking hands. When you shake hands, your right shoulder is thrust forward and your left shoulder moves out of the eye line of the other person.

If you are wearing a name tag on a lanyard, adjust the length of the string so it is positioned at the upper part of your chest. It is awkward having to move your eyes from the person's face down the person's body to the navel area to see the name tag.

✓ *Good Idea!*

Kim Miller was a new employee in a large company. She joined the company soccer team and met many new friends. She volunteered to help coordinate the holiday party. During the party, she was the master of ceremonies and introduced all the company officers at the party. This was certainly a great way to network and meet all levels of people in a new position.

✗ *Faux Pas*

Donna, the executive director of a nursing association, was the closing presenter at the annual state conference. She spent the day in her hotel room working on her presentation and checking her e-mail. Unfortunately, she missed hearing and meeting the other invited speakers. The conference-planning team wanted to invite one of the speakers to present at the national convention. Donna was unable to provide any feedback, because she had missed the chance to network with the other speakers and attendees.

What credentials should a nurse in a health care provider role wear on a name badge?

At a minimum, a registered nurse should have RN on a name badge. Patients have a right to know who is taking care of them. If you list other letters, it is your responsibility to educate others about the meaning of your credentials.

Are there cultural considerations for networking?

Yes. There are many cultural considerations, such as personal space, eye contact, topics of conversation, handshaking, and use of the business card. If you know who will be at a networking session, you should learn in advance about cultural preferences and sensitivities. For example, Chileans stand very close when talking. Chinese people may keep their eyes slightly averted as a sign of respect.

How can you disengage gracefully from a conversation?

This is important when networking, because your goal is to meet several people and not spend the entire time talking with one person. Here are some tips:

＊ Excuse yourself and say you are going to the restroom.

＊ Excuse yourself and say you have to make a phone call.

✳ Excuse yourself and say you need to touch base with a colleague.

✳ Say: "It was great speaking to you. I'll let you have some time to speak to others."

✳ Say: "It was nice meeting you. I hope to see you later."

✳ Say: "Well, Theresa, it has been nice talking with you. Will you excuse me? I see Denise over there, and I promised I'd catch up with her."

✳ Introduce the person to someone else and then excuse yourself.

Listening Skills

How can I improve my listening skills?

Listening is one of the most generous and gracious human behaviors (Krames, 2002). Never underestimate the power of good listening. A good listener can make a person feel like the most important person in the world.

2.3 **Tips for Good Listening**

Things to Do	Things to Avoid
Make good eye contact	Finishing sentences for others
Ignore distractions	Daydreaming
Smile and nod your head	Interrupting
Ask questions	Changing the subject
Face the person with your body	Distracting body language (looking around the room)
Lean forward	Looking at your watch or cell phone

Communicating With a Disabled Person

Do you have any suggestions for communicating with a person who has a disability?

Focus on the person and not on the disability. Here are some guidelines to avoid offending someone with a disability.

* Avoid using the words "victim," "cripple," or "invalid." *Disability* is preferred over *handicap*.

* Be prepared to shake hands with a person who has a *physical disability*. Note which hand he or she extends for the handshake and respond in kind.

* Identify yourself as you approach a person who has a *visual impairment*. Don't raise your voice. If the person has a guide dog, don't pet the dog without asking permission. If the person is blind, make your presence known by speaking and introducing yourself. When initiating a handshake, say something like, "May I shake your hand?" If the blind person initiates a handshake, and you cannot shake hands, explain why you can't. For example, "I'd like to shake your hand, but I am carrying several packages." Say goodbye so the person knows when you are leaving.

* If you are speaking with someone who has a *hearing impairment*, stand where you can be seen. Stay within his or her line of vision so the person can see your lips. Reduce background noise. Speak directly to the person, even if he or she has an interpreter present. Add facial expressions. Listen patiently.

* Position yourself at eye level when speaking to someone in a *wheelchair*. Never assume a person in a wheelchair cannot see, hear, or speak. Don't move a wheelchair out of reach of the person who uses it. Push a wheelchair only if the person wants your help (Brody, 2005; Mitchell, 2000).

Tips for Successful Interactions With Deaf and Hard-of-Hearing Patients

- Because deafness is an *invisible* disability, do not be embarrassed when patients tell you they are deaf or hard-of-hearing (HOH).

- Speak face to face with the patient.

- Deaf and HOH patients can do only one thing at a time. (If weighing the patient on a scale, do not ask other medical-related questions.)

- Not every deaf or HOH patient is a skilled lip reader.

- It is inappropriate and rude to use the term "deaf and dumb."

- Health care personnel should wear their name tag in the upper chest area so patients can immediately identify their name and credentials.

- According to the Americans with Disabilities Act, it is illegal for hospital personnel to ask family members to serve as interpreters to reduce expenses. A sign language interpreter should be provided upon the person's request.

- Physical touch is the normal mode of getting the attention of a deaf or HOH patient. Tap the person on the hand, arm, or shoulder to get his or her attention.

- Post a sign above the patient's hospital bed indicating that the patient is deaf or severely HOH.

- While the patient is hospitalized, nurses need to communicate to all shifts that the patient is deaf or HOH.

- If the patient rings the call bell, do not respond over the intercom.

- While in the hospital, see if closed caption television is available.

A. Kay Tyberg, HOH patient and educator

Nurse-to-Nurse Collaboration

Can you give any tips for nurse-to-nurse communication?

Civility is the key word for nurse-to-nurse communication. Nurses need to be courteous and polite with each other. Their conduct should consistently show respect for others, make others feel valued, and contribute to effective communication and team building. Uncivil behavior has a negative impact on nursing job satisfaction and turnover, as well as patient safety and outcomes (Lower, 2007).

2.4 Examples of Incivility in the Workplace

VERBAL ABUSE	NEGATIVE BEHAVIOR	PHYSICAL ABUSE
Demeaning comments	Humiliating a colleague	Throwing charts
Condescending language	Scapegoating	Assaulting someone
Making impossible demands	Withholding information	Punching a wall
Expressing impatience with questions	Undermining staff morale	Outbursts of rage
Insulting a colleague in front of a patient	Acting with a cultural bias	Slamming doors
Telling ethnic jokes	Spreading rumors	Banging into others

(Lower, 2007)

What behaviors promote positive working situations with other nurses?

Here are some ideas to promote a positive work environment:

* Greet colleagues with a smile and a "hello" when you arrive at work.

* Offer to help others.

* Thank people for helping you.

* Use polite language and good manners.

* Compliment others when appropriate.

* Avoid listening to gossip.

* Don't be a complainer.

* Respond to phone calls, e-mails, or other forms of correspondence.

* Participate in department events.

* Say "good-bye" to your co-workers when you leave the work setting.

Nurse-to-Physician Collaboration

Can you give tips for communicating with physicians on a nursing unit?

Communicating with physicians is essential for developing collaborative relationships to ensure quality patient care. Here are some tips:

* Introduce yourself and say, "I am the registered nurse taking care of _____."

* Tell the patient that the physician is on the unit. This will give the patient an opportunity to be ready and in position for an examination before the doctor enters the room. The patient will also have time to think of concerns and questions.

* Inform other nurses taking care of the physician's patients that the doctor is on the unit. This will give them time to organize their questions and concerns.

* Make rounds with the physician and discuss pertinent care issues and needed orders. If you cannot make rounds, have issues documented on a communication sheet.

* If the physician is covering for another physician, provide an update of the patient's hospital course. For example: "Mrs. Balon was admitted 3 days ago for syncope. She had a pacemaker inserted 2 days ago and is hoping to be discharged today."

* Check the orders before the physician leaves the unit and clarify as needed.

* If the physician was called to the unit to handle an urgent situation, have the physical assessment findings and updated vital signs available along with the pertinent lab values. Put the patient in a position to be examined. Discuss the concerns that led to the urgent call to the unit.

How can you demonstrate professionalism in a phone call with the physician?

This is a key area for preventing communication breakdown and acting as a patient advocate. Here are some suggestions:

* Be sure you are contacting the right physician. The orthopedic surgeon will not want to be called about an abnormal heart rate.

* Contact the physician by his or her preferred method of contact. Many physicians are using cell phones and do not want to be called on their home phone.

* If you are asking a unit clerk to initiate the call, be specific with your instructions. For example, "Please call Dr. Guisseppi at his office and say that I would like to speak to him about the blood sugar on Mike Browning."

* Be available for quick access when the call is returned. Make sure the unit clerk can quickly locate you.

* Have pertinent information at your fingertips. (For example, latest set of vital signs, intake and output, assessment data, current intravenous solutions, recent lab reports, medication list, allergy information, and patient chart.) Be succinct.

* Have an order form available and ready to use for phone orders.

Application to the Clinical Setting

Advice From a Clinical Specialty Area

Because of frequent contact with dialysis clients, nurses may reach a comfort level and disregard the professional boundary lines. Even when nurses are completely at ease with patients, they need to remember that the workplace is not their home. They should maintain a degree of formality and consider the workplace a place of respect. As an example, a colleague recounted a complaint made by her mother, who had recently begun dialysis. The staff in the dialysis unit did not call the mother by her name, but used terms such as "sweetie" and "honey." The patient found this belittling and demeaning. She was an individual with a name. This lax attitude annoyed her and made her uneasy.

(Headley, 2007)

✓ *Good Idea!*

Brian fell and fractured his patella and was admitted to the hospital for a patella repair. He started physical therapy (PT) the morning after surgery. After returning from PT, he was upset and told his nurse several reasons why he was unhappy with his treatment by the PT department.

The nurse contacted the supervisor of PT and explained his concerns. The supervisor came to the unit to discuss the problems. He was treated by a different therapist in the afternoon and was pleased with the quick response to his concerns. This situation demonstrates the nurse's role as an advocate for patients in vulnerable positions.

How can these networking and conversational tips be applied in clinical settings?

Sweat the small stuff! There is a book called *Don't Sweat the Small Stuff*. That advice does not apply in networking and clinical settings. Small things make a big difference, especially to a client in a health care setting. Some guidelines are listed below.

* Address all patients as Mr., Mrs., or Ms. Only use a first name or nickname if the patient gives you permission. Avoid all use of familiarities such as "honey" or "sweetie."

* Greet new patients with the following: "Welcome to _____. My name is (first and last name), and I am the registered nurse who will be coordinating your care until (time)."

* Review the plan of care and treatment goals for the day. Tell the patient the times of any scheduled activities, such as physical therapy. Ask for patient input.

* When leaving a patient's room, ask, "Is there anything else you need? I have the time." Make sure the call bell, phone, water, television, and tissues are within the patient's reach.

✳ When someone thanks you, replace the phrase "No problem" with "My pleasure."

✳ Many health care facilities are adopting policies and scripting to ensure more positive interactions with patients. See box below for examples.

Tips for Professional Patient Encounters

- Knock on the door, speak softly, and wait for the patient's permission to enter the room.
- Wash your hands.
- Identify the patient.
- Make eye contact and smile.
- Introduce yourself.
- Provide an explanation of what you are going to do.
- Be gentle in handling the patient.
- Ensure maximum privacy (pull the curtains and close the door).
- Wipe down the needed equipment (such as blood-pressure cuff).
- Do not act rushed even if you are.
- ASK THE PATIENT:

  How can I help you today?

  Is there anything I can get you before I leave?

  Do you have any questions?

Used with permission from Ohio Valley General Hospital, McKees Rocks, Pennsylvania

Frequently Asked Questions

 What should I do if I am talking with a colleague and someone I do not know joins us?

Introduce yourself. Your colleague may not make introductions because he or she has forgotten your name or the other person's name.

 What should I do if someone keeps asking me questions and never says anything about himself or herself?

Say, "Enough about me. Tell me about you."

 If a colleague or potential client is unavailable when I call on the phone, how can I find out a good time to call again?

In a polite manner, speak to the receptionist and say: "Can you please help me? When do you recommend that I should try calling back?"

 What should I do if I am having trouble understanding someone who is speaking English as a second language?

Ask the person to repeat what they said more slowly. Tell them you are having a hard time understanding and need their help. Put the blame on yourself and not on the speaker.

If I am speaking to someone at a reception, and a friend is waving to me across the room, what should I do?

You can wave and nod, but then return your full attention and focus on the person you are speaking with.

 What should I do if I am greeting and meeting people and I need to sneeze?

Have a handkerchief or tissue in your left hand. This way your right hand will be clean for handshakes.

 What can I do if I forget the name of someone that I need to introduce to another person?

Introduce the person you already know. For example, "I'd like you to meet Donald Smith." This will usually result in the third person introducing himself or herself. If the person does not make the introduction, you can say, "And your name is?"

 After you've met someone at a networking session, how can you keep the connection alive?

Make an effort to stay connected. For example, send notes or e-mails. Make an effort to connect within a week or two so the person can remember you. Call on the phone to say "hello" or to meet for a meal. Acknowledge any awards or honors with a congratulatory note. If you see an article that might interest the person, send it with a brief note.

 What do you do with the business cards you collect after an event?

On the back of the card, note where you met the person and any pertinent information that you want to remember. Add the date.

If you have a lot of cards, photocopy them on one or two pages. Write the date and event name on the top of the paper.

Some people have a card reader and enter them electronically into a database.

Cards can also be placed in storage sheet protectors with slots for business cards. These business card pages can hold 10 cards on a side and can be put into a binder. If you only put one card in each slot, you can read any pertinent information you wrote on the back of the card.

 What are my options if I am being introduced to someone and they sneeze into their right hand and then extend their hand for a handshake?

You can shake their hand and then go to the restroom and wash your hands. People often refer to this as "taking one for the team." Or, you can say you are getting over a cold and would prefer not to shake hands.

TAKE-AWAY TIPS

✓ The essence of networking is the building of new relationships.

✓ Successful networkers demonstrate respect, courtesy, and consideration for the feelings of others.

✓ Plan a two- or three-sentence response for the inevitable question, "What do you do?" Tailor this to the situation or event.

✓ There is nothing small about small talk.

✓ Small talk creates the foundation for developing a relationship.

✓ Update yourself on current events. It is essential to be prepared for small talk.

✓ Your name is important to you, and everyone else's name is important to him or her. Learn to remember names.

✓ One of the most important things we can give someone in a networking session is our full attention.

✓ When calling someone's office, always treat the secretary or receptionist with respect and courtesy.

✓ Make the first move when meeting new people.

✓ When someone tells you that you are a great conversationalist, it is often a compliment to your listening skills.

3

※

Appearances Are (Almost) Everything

Your Professional Presence

Do you:

Know how to look your best for a job interview?

Wonder why people question what you say?

Think you overdressed for an interview?

Think you made a bad first impression?

Want to look professional in the clinical area?

No matter what some people say, you are judged by the way you dress. Your clothes are either going to be a positive or a negative factor. *Clothes are never neutral.* If you are aware of the essentials for professional dress and body language, you can focus more on what you are saying and doing without detracting from your professional presentation.

"Clothes and manners do not make the man; but, when he is made, they greatly improve his appearance."

— Henry Ward Beecher

Professional Clothing

Do clothes really make a big difference?

Yes. Suppose you received two gifts. One gift was beautifully wrapped. The other was sloppily wrapped in cheap paper. Which gift would have the greater perceived value? Whether you are interviewing for a job, giving a presentation, or asking for a promotion, the way you dress is an important part of your overall packaging. Like gift-wrapping, the more "put together" your appearance, the more positive your impression (Whitmore, 2005).

✘ Faux Pas

Elizabeth was seeking a position as speaker for an international communications company. As part of the interviewing process, she was expected to conduct a seminar on presentation skills for business executives. Her speech evaluations were favorable, but the company evaluators made note of her wrinkled suit. She was very embarrassed and upset with the feedback about her suit. She had, in fact, been wearing an expensive suede suit that had just been dry-cleaned. This feedback caused her to rethink her professional attire. She gave away the suede suit and purchased a wool suit.

What judgments do people form about you based on your clothes?

People unconsciously judge your socioeco-
nomic status, background, level of education, and personality (Whitmore, 2005). If
you are underdressed, you can embarrass
yourself and your colleagues. If you over-
dress, you can set the wrong tone and may
intimidate others. Be aware that how you
dress makes a powerful statement about
yourself.

What impression are you giving if you wear sloppy or inappropriate attire?

This could imply that you do not respect
yourself, that you do not place value on appearance, or that you do not care that your
appearance impacts the corporate image.

How do you know the appropriate way to dress for different positions?

Look how leaders or managers dress in different positions, and model your attire to
match theirs. For example, an educator
may have a different professional look
than a corporate executive. If you are
looking to advance in your career,
dress like the people in the next
level up.

✔ Good Idea!

Jocelyn was delighted
to hear that she was the
recipient of an award
for her work with teens
in the Washington, DC,
area. The award was
to be presented at a
large banquet by a
United States senator.
Jocelyn was planning to
wear a sweater set and
slacks until she spoke
to her mother. When her
mother offered to buy a
business suit, the matter
was settled. On the day
of the award, Jocelyn
walked across the stage
looking confident and
stunning in a beautiful
suit. Most people walk
a little taller and demonstrate more confidence
when they wear a suit.

TIP

Dress for the role you aspire to.

Is professional dress more of a challenge for men or for women?

It is more of a challenge for women, because professional dress for men is more easily defined. Men look professional when they wear a suit and tie. The leeway in defining professional dress for women leads to the potential for inappropriate clothing. For example, common complaints about women in a professional setting include tight-fitting and short skirts, unprofessional hair, too much makeup, or clothing that is too casual (K.D. Pagana, 2005b).

TIP

Avoid clothes that reveal too much or leave too little to the imagination.

Do you have any tips for handbags and briefcases?

Yes, these items can detract from your overall appearance if they are shabby and worn. These articles do more than hold important papers, wallets, and cell phones. They hold clues about your professionalism, success, and personality. Think "classic" when purchasing these accessories (Whitmore, 2005).

✗ Faux Pas

Jessica purchased a sexy black dress for a cocktail party at her college reunion. She wore the same dress to the hospital's holiday party several weeks later. Unfortunately, she did not project the corporate image needed for the administrative position she had just applied for. When the committee met to discuss the applicants, several people mentioned Jessica's dress. The bottom line is that what is appropriate for wearing with friends may not be appropriate to wear in a work setting.

How can you put your best foot forward?

Make sure your shoes are in good condition. Dusty and worn-looking shoes detract from a professional appearance. Shoes are often assessed to evaluate your attention to detail.

 Tips for Professional Dress for Women

Suit colors	Navy blue, charcoal gray, black, burgundy, and taupe are traditional.
	Wear darker hues during the winter.
	Wear colors that are flattering to your skin tone.
Suit fabrics	Buy fabrics that wear well.
	Wool knits, crepes, and microfibers generally wrinkle less.
	Linens are known for wrinkling.
Blouses	Avoid blouses that are too revealing.
	Only wear a sleeveless blouse under a suit.
Scarves	Silk and silk blends hang better than cotton.
	The classic size is 34 inches square.
	Scarves can soften a tailored look.

Tips for Professional Dress
for Women   (continued)

Shoes	The classic pump has a 1 to 1½ inch heel.
	Spiked heels (3 inches or higher) and flat heels look least professional.
	Business colors are black, navy, brown, and taupe.
	Don't wear shoes that are scuffed or have worn-down heels.
Boots	Boots can be acceptable for classic business dress in some settings.
	Avoid having a gap between the bottom of your skirt and the boot tops.
Stockings	Neutral or flesh tones are always smart.
	Do not wear dark stockings with light shoes.
Belts	The classic width is ½ to ¾ inch.
	Leather belts should coordinate with your shoes.
	If metal, match it to other metal (earrings, necklaces, buttons, watch).
Jewelry	Your jewelry should accent, not dominate, your outfit.
	Earrings should be compatible in size to necklaces.
	Wear one ring per hand. (Wedding and engagement rings count as one.)
Watches	Match the metal of your watch to your other jewelry.

Tips for Professional Dress for Women (continued)	
Eyeglasses	Wear updated frames.
	Don't let your glasses compete with your jewelry.
	Match the metal of your glasses to your other jewelry.
Purses	The purse should be neat and functional.
	A poorly made or worn-out purse can downgrade your outfit.
	Coordinate your briefcase with your purse.

(Brody, 2005; Post & Post, 1999)

How do you know what colors are flattering for you?

Hold a piece of clothing up to your face and study how you look. A flattering color will make your eye color more intense and your skin tone more vibrant, and will give you an energetic look. In contrast, your skin will look sallow, your eyes dull, and your face tired with an unflattering color (Post & Post, 1999). Many professionals have dramatically improved their appearance with the help of an image consultant.

What about makeup?

Most women look better with a little makeup. The key is to use makeup to enhance, not to dominate. Make sure there is no lipstick on your teeth.

What about professional women with long hair?

Hair should be kept out of the eyes. It can be tucked behind the ears, pulled back with a barrette, pulled up in a ponytail, or twisted up with a clamp.

3.2	Tips for Professional Dress for Men	
Suit colors	Navy blue, gray, and black are the business standards.	
	Dark colors are associated with more authority.	
Suit fabrics	Wool is the fabric of choice.	
	The suit surface should be matte, not shiny.	
Slacks	Pants fitted to the waist are more slimming.	
	Flat fronts are more slimming than pleats.	
	Cuffs are more classic in style than pants without cuffs.	
Dress shirts	White is the dressiest.	
	Shades of blue, gray, tan, and muted green are preferred.	
	The point collar looks fine open or with a tie.	
	Always wear a tie with spread collars.	
	Don't wear a tie with short-sleeve shirt.	

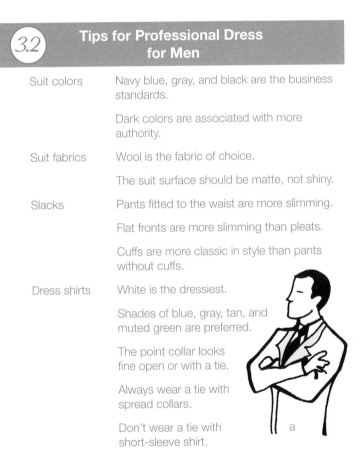
a

Tips for Professional Dress for Men (continued)

Shoes	Shoes should harmonize with the outfit.
	Wear black shoes with gray, navy, or black suits.
	Wear brown shoes with tan, brown, or beige suits.
Socks	Match socks with your pants.
	Exception: With tan pants, socks should match the shoes.
	Socks should be high enough to cover the shins when sitting.
Ties	Silk is the best fabric.
	The tie should complement the suit color, but not match it.
	Wear a wider tie with a wider lapel.
	Wear a thinner tie with a slimmer lapel.
	The tip of the tie should end at the top or middle of the belt.
Belts	Match the belt to your shoe color.
	The standard belt width is 1¼ inches.
Jewelry	Keep your jewelry subtle and minimal.
	Do not wear more than one ring per hand.
	Match metal to metal with jewelry items (for example, gold to gold).
Eyeglasses	Wear updated frames.
	A round face looks better with square frames.
	A square face looks better with round frames.

Tips for Professional Dress for Men (continued)	
Wallets	Dark leather is the most traditional.
	The wallet should be thin and not cause a bulge in the back pocket.
Miscellaneous	When wearing a single-breasted suit or sports coat, button the top button when you stand. Unbutton it when you sit down.

(Brody, 2005; Post & Post, 1999)

Dressing in the Clinical Setting

"Know first who you are; and then adorn yourself accordingly."

—Euripides

What impact does dress have in a clinical setting?

Dress has a bigger impact than most nurses realize. The way you dress supports or detracts from your professional image. It sends a message to others about how you see yourself and how you want to be perceived by others. It sets the stage for what others may expect from you. Most nurses would agree that they would like to be viewed as professional, intelligent, and competent. They need to ask themselves if their appearance mirrors that image.

If nurses dress too casually, patients may question their attention to detail and their professionalism. Patients often associate appearance with trustworthiness and ability. Does a nurse dressed in bunny print scrubs establish immediate trust, authority, and credibility? Many patients complain that everyone in a clinical setting looks the same. Patients want their nurses to be clearly identifiable. This identification is also essential for having positive interactions with families, physicians, and other members of the health team.

Nurses in White

If you are a patient at St. Clair Hospital in Pittsburgh, you can clearly identify your nurse. Nurses wear white uniforms or white scrubs. Nurse aides wear white bottoms with green tops. Joan Massella, chief nursing officer, said the change was done for two major reasons. First, many nurses did not appear professional due to their style of dress. Second, it was done to improve patient satisfaction. The majority of patients were elderly and could not differentiate nurses from other hospital employees.

Do the nurses like the change? According to Joan, not all of them are happy, but they look great. Do the patients like the change? Yes, the patients and their family members like being able to identify their nurses.

Can scrubs be part of a professional image?

Many hospitals are re-evaluating their dress codes. Scrubs may be on their way out, as the credibility and professionalism of health care personnel are under scrutiny.

According to image consultant Sandy Dumont (personal communication, 2007), uniforms are necessary for professional identification. In her opinion, nurses look most professional when wearing white. She believes that hospitals need to mandate dress codes. If they permit scrubs, she asserts that there should be uniformity. All nurses should wear the same color, so it doesn't look like someone was hired off the street and doesn't have a uniform yet.

Notes From an Image Consultant

It's a matter of life and death, and you show up wearing "pink pajamas" with cartoon motifs. How is a patient to know that you're not there to change the bedpans? Nothing about your appearance announces that you are a highly educated expert who is a member of an honored profession.

If you boarded an airplane and the co-pilot greeted you wearing a polo shirt and khakis, while the pilot wore the traditional uniform, would you be taken aback? Would you assume that the casually dressed pilot was still in training, or that perhaps he was called in to fly at a moment's notice? "Hope he wasn't drinking the night before," you might say to yourself. Furthermore, what would you think about the airline that permitted pilots to dress for their own comfort, rather than wear a proper uniform?

Don't cheat your patients of their expectation to be cared for by a highly educated expert who is a member of an honored profession. If you are proud of who you are and what you do, shout it to the world by *looking* like a nurse!

Sandy Dumont is an image consultant with 30 years' experience. She conducts workshops and seminars throughout the country and abroad. Contact her and get a free book at her Web site: www.theimagearchitect.com.

What are some general guidelines for dress in the clinical setting?

All nurses in all settings should look neat and professional. Uniforms, lab coats, scrubs, and shoes should be clean. Long hair should be pulled back and out of the face. Name tags should be visible and readable.

✗ Faux Pas

As part of hospital orientation, a clinical group of nursing students was told about the hospital and university dress code policy. On clinical days, they were to wear their uniforms and lab coats. But, while pre-planning, they could wear business casual clothes with their lab coats and name tags. One week later, two of the students arrived for pre-planning wearing soccer shorts, tee shirts, and flip-flops. They were not permitted on the unit, and the negative impression they left stuck with them. The staff referred to them as the "soccer girls" for the rest of the semester.

Body Language

What impact does body language have on the overall impression a person makes?

We communicate with each other visually, vocally, and verbally. The professional impression we provide is based on the words we use (verbal), the way our voice sounds (vocal), and what people see (visual). The visual element has the strongest impact and consists of everything people see when they look at you. This includes your dress, grooming, and body language.

The care and time you invest in your appearance and words can be undone by body language. For example, suppose you are dressed in a professional manner, but you are slouching and leaning back in your chair. You are probably sending a message that you are not as interested as you should be.

"When the eyes say one thing, and the tongue another, a practiced man relies on the language of the first."

—Ralph Waldo Emerson

✓ *Good Idea!*

Kristin was teaching a workshop on time management. The workshop was videotaped so it could be shown for evening and night shift personnel. When Kristin viewed her tape, she was disappointed. She had an unpleasant look on her face, and her posture was poor. Her body language detracted from her professionalism. She used this feedback in a constructive manner and greatly improved her presentation skills. Most people would benefit by critiquing themselves on videotape.

How can you tell if your body language is having a negative impact on your professionalism?

Tune in and be aware of what image your nonverbal communication is projecting. Many negative aspects of body language are bad habits that can be corrected with awareness. Get feedback from others.

(3.3)	Body Language Tips
Standing	Stand tall with your shoulders back and your chin up.
	Keep your shoulders relaxed.
	Avoid slouching, swaying, and shifting your feet.
	Don't keep your hands in your pockets.
	Folding your arms may denote defensiveness or disagreement.
	Don't put your hands on your hips.
Sitting	Sit up straight.
	Keep legs together, especially when wearing a skirt.
	Avoid slouching.
	Don't jiggle your knees or tap your feet.

Body Language Tips

Facial expressions	A sincere smile denotes warmth and friendliness.
	A false smile makes you look phony.
	A frown makes you look angry or worried.
	Be animated, but don't overdo.
Eye contact	Looking at the eyes of another shows your interest.
	Occasionally look away and move your eyes to another part of the face.
	Don't stare or shift your eyes.
Gestures	Use gestures to make a point.
	Vary your gestures.
	Gesture with open hands.
	Don't wring your hands, point, or make a fist.
	Don't overdo gesturing.
	Avoid the following: playing with your hair or jewelry, biting your lips, twisting your mustache, drumming your fingers, clicking pens, picking your teeth, biting your fingernails, jiggling keys or change in your pocket.
Movement	Move with confidence and purpose.
	Don't drag or shuffle your feet.

(Pachter, 2006b; Post & Post, 1999)

Frequently Asked Questions

 Is it better to be overdressed or underdressed in a new work setting?

In general, it is better to err on the more formal side. Remember, you can always remove a jacket, but you cannot put one on if you didn't bring it with you.

 If I am dressed inappropriately, couldn't it mean that I just did not know any better?

Yes. But, that is not an excuse. You need to find out the appropriate dress. By your inappropriate dress, you could also be suggesting that you do not care what others think or that you are too lazy to make the effort to dress better.

 Why are corporate casual dress codes being eliminated in many settings?

The informality gave many people the impression that there were no guidelines or boundaries between dressing for work and relaxing at home. This had a negative impact on professional image and work ethic.

 Is it acceptable for men to wear baseball caps inside?

No. It is considered bad manners. Men should remove hats when entering a place of business or entering a room.

 Do you have any tips for men wearing suspenders?

Suspenders should be matched to the tie. The subdued or flashy pattern should be compatible with the company culture.

What about tattoos?

Keep them hidden, if possible. Don't get tattoos on your hand or face. The tattoo becomes part of your image and may hurt your chance of getting a job or getting promoted.

 Is it professional for men or women to wear cologne or perfume in the work setting?

Subtlety is the key. Remember you are not an air freshener. Moderation is best. If people comment about your cologne in the afternoon, you are using too much. If your scent lingers in a room after you've left, you are using too much. Be sensitive to the fact that many people are allergic to cologne or perfume.

TAKE-AWAY TIPS

✓ **You will have a better chance of feeling good on the inside if you look good on the outside.**

✓ **Dress for the job you aspire to, not for the job you have.**

✓ **Wear clothes that fit well. Invest in a good tailor or seamstress.**

✓ **Your clothes impact your credibility.**

✓ **Don't wear sunglasses or hats inside.**

✓ **Sloppy clothing may imply sloppy work.**

4

✳

Interviewing

What You Say Gets You What You Want!

Do you:

Know what to expect during an interview?

Know what to wear?

Know what to bring?

Know what to do if you are asked a question you can't answer?

Know how to react to the unexpected?

Are you:

Nervous before and during an interview?

A less-than-stellar interviewee?

These are legitimate concerns that can add to the normal stress of an interview. The trick is to know how to prepare and present yourself so you can minimize anxiety and maximize your level of confidence.

This chapter provides guidelines to support you in any interview or even any business meeting.

Preparing for the Interview

What should I do before the interview?

Find out as much as you can about the company or position.

X *Faux Pas*

John did a great job promoting himself for a cardiovascular sales position in a pharmaceutical company. He eloquently described his various job positions related to cardiac nursing. Unfortunately, when asked about the company's new cardiac drug that had received FDA approval a few weeks earlier, he could not answer the question. One look at the company's Web site would have informed him of this drug's approval and helped him to prepare himself accordingly.

Check the Web site for information about the company and people in charge. The more you find out, the more prepared you will be and feel. It's also important to review your public persona. Prospective employers may search the Web for information on you and may locate your Web site, blog, or social networking profile (Facebook or MySpace, for example). Make sure there is nothing there (words or pictures) that could embarrass you or your potential employer.

Is it a good idea to have some names to drop?

Talk to family, friends, and people on the street, train, or bus. See if you can get a name to drop. Leverage those you know. When used appropriately, personal connections can allow you to walk through a door opened wide, rather than just let you get a foot in the door.

Try to familiarize yourself with names. If you are applying for a teaching position, learn the names of faculty members. Review their Web sites. If you can't pronounce a name, call the department secretary and ask.

Do you know anyone with inside contacts?

If so, talk to them before the interview about the position. What kind of personalities fit well in the job culture? What are the hidden expectations for employees? Why do people stay and why do they leave?

TIP

People like to do business with people they know and like. Responsible name-dropping can take you from the position of "stranger" to "insider" in the blink of an eye.

Who will be at the interview?

Call the person who scheduled you for the interview. Explain that you want to be as prepared as possible, and ask if he or she can tell you what to expect and who will be there. Find out the title of each interviewer and his or her role in the organization. This will help you direct questions to the appropriate person.

Often, you will be able to get biographical information on the Web site. See if you have any commonalities. If so, bring them up during the interview. For example, perhaps you went to the same college, did the same nursing internship, or both served in the Army Nurse Corps.

What are some of the questions that may be asked?

The bulleted list below offers sample questions you may encounter. Role-play your response in fewer than 2 minutes. It may be a good idea to write out your responses. Practice answering these questions out loud. Practice will help you sound more confident and avoid filler words and sounds such as "you know" and "um." Be sure to allow time for spontaneous comments.

* Describe what attracted you to the nursing profession.

* What experiences do you have that will help you in this position?

* What distinguishes you from other job candidates?

* What are your major strengths?

* What are your major weaknesses?

* Describe a difficult problem you faced in the past and how you resolved it.

* Tell me about a time when you learned to get along with a difficult person.

* Contrast a good decision with a poor decision you've made.

* How do you react to stressful situations?

* Where do you see yourself in 3-5 years?

* Have you ever coached or worked with a group where you had to help people less experienced than yourself?

* What experiences have you had working in teams?

✗ Faux Pas

At the end of a job interview, Ryan asked the interviewer how best to follow up on the hiring decision. When the interviewer gave Ryan a phone number to call, Ryan asked if he could borrow a pen and piece of paper to write it down. The first thing the interviewer did once Ryan left was to make a note to himself: "Candidate was disorganized and did not even bring a pen and piece of paper."

Professionalism During the Interview

What should I bring to the interview?

Bring a portfolio or folder with appropriate materials. For example, if you were asked to bring a professional license, make sure you have it in the folder. At the very least, bring:

* List of questions for the interviewer(s)

* Pad of paper or notebook for making notes or taking down follow-up information

* A writing utensil and a spare, in case the first gets lost or damaged

* 5-10 professional-looking copies of your résumé

"The apparel oft proclaims the man."

—Shakespeare (from *Hamlet*)

X Faux Pas

Mary had worked in a hospital and was used to wearing scrubs. When she interviewed with a pharmaceutical company, she thought wearing a sweater set would be fine. She was embarrassed when she saw that she was the only one not wearing a suit. It is always better for clothing to be more formal than too casual. This shows respect for the interviewer and demonstrates that you made the effort to present yourself in a professional manner.

✓ *Good Idea!*

Monica was finishing her junior year of college and applying for summer internships. She recently attended a seminar about business etiquette and thought she needed to purchase a suit for her interviews. Because her mother disagreed with her, Monica e-mailed the seminar speaker to specifically ask about the suit. The speaker supported Monica's position and reviewed the reasons for purchasing a suit. Monica felt confident and professional in her suit, did great during her interviews, and was offered the internship she wanted.

What should I wear to the interview?

Wear a dark suit unless you were advised to wear something else. Avoid yellow, red, or pink suits. However, these colors are fine for accessories or accent pieces. Stay away from long, dangling jewelry. Some human resource experts recommend the "rule of five" for jewelry. This limits jewelry to five pieces, such as two rings, a watch, earrings, and a necklace.

Make sure the suit fits well and all accessories match. Clothing is never neutral. It either adds to or detracts from your appearance.

Shoes are important too. For men, leather soles are best. Before the week of your interview, try on the suit to make sure your shoes are the right height. Give yourself time in case you need alterations in length or different shoes. Even if employees dress casually, job seekers are expected to dress more formally. This shows you are taking the interview seriously and you respect the company.

Make sure your hygiene is flawless. A wrinkled shirt, food caught in your teeth, or chipped fingernails can detract from your professional impression.

What about body piercings and tattoos?

"We don't care what you have pierced or tattooed, as long as we don't see it" is a common stand on body art and piercings. Limit any visible piercing to the earlobes and keep tattoos covered, if possible. Remove the jewelry item from piercings that cannot be covered (pierced tongue, eyebrow ring).

 Appearance and Hygiene Checklist

Men:

Freshly bathed and shaven (even if interview is later in the day)

Clean fingernails

Deodorant applied

Teeth brushed

Clean, ironed clothes

Shoes polished

Minimal amount of cologne

Women:

Freshly bathed

Clean, manicured fingernails

Deodorant applied

No excessive jewelry, makeup, or perfume

Wearing a bra with no underwear showing

Clean, ironed clothes

Clothes that are not too tight, too sexy, or too short

Shoes polished

Is it OK to smoke while waiting for an interview?

Absolutely not. If you smoke, try not to before the interview, because your clothing will reek of cigarette smoke. That is a definite turnoff for many people. Don't smoke anywhere inside or outside of the facility.

How can I be sure I'm on time for the interview?

Drive to the location before the day of the interview whenever possible, and plan your best route to avoid potential traffic pitfalls. Find where to park and note the entrance to the building. This will eliminate a major stress on the interview day.

Allow extra time for traffic and accidents on the day of the interview. Make sure you have all relevant phone numbers with you. If you are caught in a traffic jam, call your contact and notify him or her that you may be late. Tell the person you will call back with an update. Always plan to arrive at least 30 minutes early. Bring a professional or other business-based magazine or book to read while waiting. This will demonstrate that you are serious about continuing to learn and improve professionally.

Allow time to use the restroom and check your appearance before presenting yourself to the receptionist 5 to 10 minutes ahead of time. Be sure to greet the receptionist with courtesy and respect. The receptionist may be asked to comment on your behavior and manners. Wait for the receptionist to advise you on where to sit.

✗ Faux Pas

There was a buzz in the hallway outside one of the meeting rooms after a presentation. The female speaker had worn a white suit. Her red underwear could be seen through her suit, which distracted the audience from listening to her presentation. Her clothes undermined her professionalism and expertise.

Interview: Dos and Don'ts

Do:

Use a firm handshake.

Wait to be offered a seat.

Have good eye contact with interviewer(s).

Maintain good posture.

Speak so you can be easily heard, but not too loudly.

Be direct and to the point without rambling.

Don't:

Use a limp or crushing handshake.

Chew gum.

Sit down until you are directed to do so.

Give one-word answers.

Give long, drawn-out answers.

Interrupt anyone who is speaking.

Bad-mouth a previous employer.

Order an alcoholic beverage if you are taken to lunch.

Comment about nationality, age, religion, or photographs of family or children.

X *Faux Pas*

Peg received several long-distance calls on her answering machine from a hospital, asking her for a reference. Because Peg was unaware of anyone interviewing who might use her for a reference, she did not return the calls. A week later, she ran into a former student who mentioned she had applied for an out-of-state job and had listed Peg as a reference. If the former student had contacted her sooner, Peg would have immediately returned the call to show her enthusiastic support of the applicant.

The polite way to handle this situation is to ask permission before listing someone as a reference. Even if you have previously received a person's permission to use him or her as a reference, it is important to contact the person before any new job search to be sure nothing has changed.

Should I come prepared with some questions?

Yes, this shows careful preparation. Here are two good questions to ask:

1. What skills are considered most important for success in this position?

2. What kind of educational opportunities do you offer to support career growth?

During an interview, is it OK to ask when you can expect to hear about the position?

Yes, this is a reasonable question. You may say: "I am confident that I would do a good job. What is the next step in the selection process?"

What should I do at the end of the interview?

Shake hands and thank the interviewer(s). Say goodbye to the receptionist. Remember his or her name. If someone walks you out, this is still part of the interview. Be careful of what you say.

Maintain professional behavior and manners as you exit and get into your car. Don't light up a cigarette or take off your jacket as you walk out of the building.

"Clothes are never a frivolity: They always mean something."

—James Laver

Things Not to Say in an Interview

"Do you have a smoking area?"

Smoking is a turnoff. Medical insurance may be higher for smokers.

"I'm not sure what to do with my kids if I get this job."

This suggests you may have child-care problems.

"I really need this job to get away from my home situation."

This is too personal and could affect your ability to perform your job effectively.

"This city has great bars!"

Will you have a hangover on Monday?

"Are those pictures of your children?"

It is inappropriate to discuss children, regardless of whose children they are, in interviews. The conversation could lead into delicate or possibly illegal areas and may make the interviewer uncomfortable.

"Do you have disability insurance?"

The interviewer may wonder if you are trying to get a job in order to go out on a disability claim. It is illegal to discriminate against anyone with disabilities.

Marianne P. Deska, human resources consultant

After-Interview Professionalism

Should I write a thank-you note after the interview?

Yes. A thank-you note will make you stand out and be remembered. Compose a short handwritten note, and write clearly and neatly. Two short, typed paragraphs are standard for a business position. Try to mention one thing you had in common with the interviewer or someone in the desired position—for example, you both went to the same university. Mail the note within 24 hours of the interview. Only e-mail a thank-you note if you are following it with a mailed note.

The note will usually be placed in your application file. When files are reviewed, this will reflect positively on your manners and people skills.

Typed thank-you note

August 15, 2008

Dear Ms. Nardi,

Thank you for meeting with me today. I am very interested in the nursing position on the orthopedic unit. With my certification in orthopedic nursing and my experience with joint replacements, I believe I would be an asset to the unit.

It was a pleasure meeting you. Please let me know if you need any more information. Thanks again for your time and consideration.

Sincerely,

Margaret K. McDermott, BSN, RN

Handwritten thank-you note

August 15. 2008
Dear Ms. Nardi.

Thank you for meeting w
in the nursing position on
tification in orthopedic
replacements. I believe

It was a ple
if you need any mor
time and considerati

Top 10 Interview Blunders

1. Making negative comments about former employers, supervisors, or co-workers. (No matter how bad they were, bashing them NEVER makes you look good!)

2. Giving a call-back number that leads to an unprofessional outgoing voice-mail message, or using an inappropriate e-mail address. (No loud music, toddlers attempting to say "Mommy/Daddy isn't home," or slang. Remember that your e-mail address can reveal a lot about you. It's worth the extra effort to create a professional e-mail address for job searches.)

3. Wearing inappropriate attire. (Flip-flops, plunging necklines, exposed thongs, sweatshirts, or spandex material of any kind is never appropriate. If you have to ask yourself or someone else, "Does this look OK?" then it most likely doesn't.)

4. Arriving too early or too late. (Arriving late obviously sends a bad message, but arriving more than 20 minutes early can send a bad message as well—it's annoying.)

5. Divulging too much personal information. (No matter how much you want or need the position, do not dissolve into tears about your marriage woes or child-care issues. This will not help you get the job.)

6. Cell phone interruptions. (Even in vibrate mode, a cell phone going off is still a distraction and potentially sends the signal that you will be taking too many personal phone calls. Always turn off your cell phone!)

7. Incomplete or incorrect contact information on résumé or application. (Take time to update former employer and reference information.)

8. Inability to speak about or recognize past mistakes or weaknesses. (Everyone drops the ball sometime. Be prepared to talk about it and explain how you grew from the experience.)

9. Bringing friends, children, or significant others with you to an interview. (You'll be expected to perform your job without their support. Having them there will be unprofessional and can make you appear too eager and needy.)

10. Lack of enthusiasm. (This is especially bad for a new graduate. A winning attitude and desire to learn can easily make up for lack of practical experience.)

Nicole Nardi, BSN, RN, nurse recruiter

If I haven't heard about the position in the time anticipated, what should I do?

Call and say that you are "checking in" about the status of your application.

If I get a rejection letter or find out the position was filled, should I call and ask why I didn't get the position?

No. Send a letter saying that you know the position was filled. Tell them you are interested in other related positions. This keeps your name in the forefront and shows that you are not a "poor loser."

Phone Interviews

What is the main purpose of a phone interview?

Phone interviews are a cost-effective, timesaving method for screening job candidates. Your goal for a phone interview is to get an invitation for an in-person interview. See the following list for guidelines to ensure a successful interview.

Guidelines for a Phone Interview

* Prepare as you would for a personal interview. Because there is no chance for eye contact or other nonverbal cues, you need to be impeccably prepared. This is your only chance to make a first impression.

* Control your surroundings. You must be able to talk freely without any distracting background noises. No crying kids or blaring televisions.

* Get into a business mode. Many people dress professionally because they feel and act more businesslike during the interview.

* Stand up. Your voice will sound more confident and dynamic.

* Smile. The smile on your face can be heard in your voice and projects a positive impression.

* Have a pen and paper available. Take notes. Ask questions.

* Have your résumé and supporting data in front of you. You may be asked questions about your background and previous experiences.

* Be a good listener. You want to gather information to see if you are a fit for the organization.

* Turn off the call-waiting option on your phone.

* Watch your manners. Use the person's title. Don't chew gum or smoke.

* Close the interview. Ask about the next step in the interview process.

* Send a thank-you note after the interview (K.D. Pagana, in press b).

Frequently Asked Questions

 How can I get correct names and titles of interviewer(s) for writing thank-you notes?

Ask for a business card, check the Web site, or call the office. If you call the office, say you are writing thank-you notes and want to be certain that you have correct names and titles.

What should I do with my coat?

Take it off before you get to the interview area. Fold it over your left arm so your right hand is free for shaking hands. Ask the receptionist where to hang it.

If there is candy on the table, is it OK to take a piece?

No. You want to be free to talk without food in your mouth.

May I bring a water bottle into the interview?

No. Don't put anything on the interviewer's desk. If there is a table in front of you, you may put your interview folder on it.

What if I am asked a question that I cannot answer?

Think about it for a few seconds. Then, simply say, "I don't know" or "I can't answer that question." Don't apologize. If you know where or how to find the answer, you can explain that. This demonstrates your resourcefulness.

Is it OK to ask about salary in the first interview?

No, it is better to focus on getting the interviewer interested in you and wanting you for the position. Save the salary question for subsequent interviews.

What if I am asked about salary?

Do your homework before the interview so you know what this type of position pays. Say you are looking for something in the salary range that is appropriate for the position.

Should I ask permission before listing someone as a reference?

Yes, ask the person if he or she is willing to serve as a reference. Then send a thank-you note and a copy of your résumé so the person will be up-to-date on your job situation.

What should I say when an interviewer asks about my major weakness?

Mention an area related to the job, but not required for the position you are applying for. For example, suppose you are applying for a teaching position in medical-surgical nursing. You could say, "I have several ideas for articles, but I have not published anything yet. I am planning to attend a writing and publishing workshop later this year."

May I ask about advancement opportunities?

Yes, but be careful you don't give the impression you are too ambitious and are mentally planning your next career-advancement move.

Is it OK to talk about interviewing with other companies?

Yes, but be careful. It may be better not to mention other companies until you are discussing salary or you are asked, as opposed to bringing it up yourself. Leveraging your situation with other interviews is a great way to make you seem more desirable. If the interviewer is worried about losing you to a competitor, your bargaining position can improve.

TAKE-AWAY TIPS

✓ **Grandma's right: You never get a second chance to make a good first impression.**

✓ **Dress for the role you aspire to.**

✓ **Turn your cell phone off before your interview. If it goes off by mistake, apologize and quickly turn it off without answering it.**

✓ **Never bad-mouth former employers during the interview.**

✓ **Answer the employer's questions in 20 seconds to 2 minutes.**

✓ **You can increase your chances of getting a job by projecting a positive, upbeat, confident, and mature attitude during interviews.**

✓ **Ask the interviewer for a business card. This will give you the correct spelling of the name, the proper title, and the address for writing a thank-you note.**

✓ **Sending a thank-you note demonstrates good people skills.**

5

*

Controlling Technology Before It Controls You

Communication Technology

Do you:

Know what to do if your cell phone rings during a meeting?

Want to demonstrate professionalism on a conference call?

Wonder if you should fax or mail a key document?

Know if you should use an electronic signature?

Know what to do if your e-mail system does not have a spell-check feature?

With today's technology, opportunity rarely knocks anymore. Instead, it presents itself in the form of a phone call or a voice mail or e-mail message. Technology is fast, efficient, and inexpensive. However convenient and efficient these forms of communication are, they can be annoying, intrusive, and rude. It is easy to abuse communication devices such as personal digital assistants (PDAs), cell-phone text messaging, e-mail, and instant messaging. This abuse can be costly to careers. If you want to present yourself in a courteous and professional manner, use techno-etiquette with all forms of correspondence.

"Politeness and consideration for others is like investing pennies and getting dollars back."

—Thomas Sowell

E-mail Etiquette

Why does e-mail have a large impact on professionalism?

E-mail is now used more than any other type of communication. Whatever you write could come back to haunt you. Even deleted messages can be retrieved. Therefore, blunders become permanent. See Table 5.1 for some key tips to make e-mail work *for* you instead of *against* you.

Key Tips for Using E-mail

* Don't send confidential information. Ever. This information is one "forward" away from someone who may choose to use it against you or your company.

* Make the subject line specific. This helps the reader prioritize messages.

* Include a greeting and a close. It is more polite and less impersonal.

* Use short paragraphs.

* Don't use all capital letters. They are considered the same as shouting.

* Don't use all lowercase letters. They make you look lazy.

* Use your e-mail software's built-in grammar tool and spell check. Proofread before sending.

* Maintain a business tone. Never use inappropriate language.

* Check your recipients before sending. This will avoid many errors.

* Avoid overuse of "reply all." This annoys people.

* Check your e-mail regularly.

* Confirm your receipt of e-mails containing important information.

* Respond to e-mails within 24 hours.

* Don't forward chain letters or anything else you would not want to receive (K.D. Pagana, 2007b; K.D. Pagana, 2007c).

 *Faux Pas*

A pharmaceutical representative was not happy with a secretary's help with his program set-up at a hospital. After the program, he sent an angry e-mail to the secretary that contained some foul language. The secretary forwarded it to the hospital president, who e-mailed the representative and permanently prohibited him from being on hospital grounds.

Should your e-mail include a signature block?

Yes. The signature block should include your name, address, phone number, fax number, and e-mail address. This provides several ways to contact you. Your address provides people with information necessary to identify your time zone, so they know when they can call you.

Setting up an e-mail signature is easy to do. For example, if you are using Microsoft Outlook, go to the Tools drop-down menu and select Options. From there, select the Mail Format tab and click on Signatures. If you do not have Outlook, use your help feature and type in "signature," or ask your information technology (IT) support staff for assistance.

What is the recommended length of an e-mail message?

Keep it short. Try to keep the entire message viewable without scrolling. Long messages can be tedious. Keeping messages short is especially helpful for people who check their messages on a PDA such as the BlackBerry®. Use the phone for long messages.

What should you do if your e-mail system does not have a grammar and spell-check tool?

Copy the material and move it into your word processing program. Check the grammar and spelling and then move the text back into your e-mail message.

Is there an acceptable way to forward messages?

Don't forward messages with pages of "mail-to" information. Delete all extraneous information such as addresses and date lines.

How can I avoid forgetting to add an attachment?

As soon as you mention an attachment, insert it before finishing your sentence or beginning the next sentence. This will prevent having to send a second e-mail with an apology and the attachment.

If you are sending several attachments, find out if the recipient wants to receive them separately or all in one e-mail. Multiple attachments may slow down the recipient's incoming messages.

Is it best to include one topic in each e-mail?

Yes. This makes it easier for people to respond and easier to file the e-mail. If this is not possible, number your items to simplify the response.

When should you use the BCC?

Use the blind carbon copy (BCC) when sending a message to multiple addresses. People do not like having their e-mail addresses broadcast to everyone on your list. Put your name in the "To" box and the rest of the names in the BCC box. You should not give out someone's e-mail address without permission.

It is not necessary to use the BCC when corresponding with a work team. These people know each other and probably already have other recipients' e-mail addresses. In this case, put all of the addresses on the "To" line.

Should you use an auto-responder or out-of-the-office assistant when you are unavailable?

This is a good idea when you will be unavailable for a period of time. People won't wonder if you received their e-mails. It will also tell them when you will return.

What factors should you consider when setting up an e-mail address?

Make sure it is professional. Here are some examples to avoid:

> "mamabear@ ..."
>
> "sexymama@ ..."
>
> "billysmom@ ..."

Cute or clever e-mail addresses may be appropriate for personal messaging or social networking sites, but they are not appropriate for professional work. Use your full name whenever possible, and be sure to set up your e-mail address display to show your full name on outgoing mail. (If you don't know how to set up your e-mail address, go to the Help utility tool in your e-mail software.)

Are there situations when you should not use e-mail?

Yes. Here are some examples:

* Resigning from a job.

* Discussing sensitive or confidential information.

* Sending urgent information without follow-up. (Computer glitches can happen.)

* When you need an immediate response. Use the phone instead (K.D. Pagana, 2007c).

Telephone & Speakerphone Etiquette

How can you communicate your professionalism on the telephone?

The sound of your voice and your manners are essential components of phone etiquette. Smile, because the smile on your face comes through in your voice. Immediately identify yourself. Never assume someone will recognize your voice. Keep your full attention on the person with whom you are speaking. See Table 5.2 for some tips.

5.2 Telephone Tips

* Keep background noises to a minimum.

* Concentrate on listening and avoid multi-tasking.

* Try to return calls within 24 hours.

* Get yourself organized before placing a call.

* Schedule phone conversations to avoid playing phone tag.

* Put callers on hold only when necessary. Ask for permission before placing them on hold.

* Don't answer your phone if you have a visitor in your office.

* Don't use call waiting in business situations.

Telephone Tips   (continued)

* Avoid calling when you expect your contact to be busy.

* When returning someone's call, consider his or her time zone.

What is the best way to transfer a call?

Always tell the caller the extension in case you are disconnected during the transfer. Brief the recipient about the caller so he or she can be prepared for the call (Brody, 2005).

What is the polite way to conclude a business phone call?

TIP

Courtesy begets courtesy.

The person who initiated the call should bring it to a close. If not, the other person can politely ask if there is anything else to be settled. End on a positive note with a comment such as, "It's been nice talking to you," or "Thanks for your help with this project." Then, say goodbye and gently hang up the phone.

Do you have any suggestions for using speakerphones?

Yes. See Table 5.3 for tips to avoid blunders.

Tips to Avoid Speakerphone Blunders

✳ Only use speakerphones when you are on a conference call.

✳ Identify yourself when you begin to speak.

✳ Identify everyone in the room who will be participating in the call.

✳ Don't carry on any side conversations during a conference call.

✳ Tell your listeners if you have to leave during the call.

✳ Don't use your speakerphone for listening to your voice mail. It is annoying to others who can hear it and could be embarrassing to the person who left a message intended only for your ears.

✳ Always ask permission before putting someone on a speakerphone.

What can you do if you suspect someone has put you on a speakerphone?

If you are uncomfortable, say something like, "I'm having trouble hearing you. Would you take me off your speakerphone?" The other person will usually pick up the handset (Pachter, 2006a).

What is the proper etiquette for using caller identification?

You should use caller identification only to prepare for a call by identifying its source. It can create confusion and throw people off guard when they are greeted by name without having a chance to identify themselves.

Good Idea!

Matt finished graduate school and was interviewing for jobs in nursing administration. Before sending out résumés, he added a signature block to his e-mail and updated his voice mail message to make it more professional. He got rid of the music that preceded his message. He also Googled himself to make sure he would not be embarrassed by anything that an interviewer could find out about him on the Internet. (A growing number of hiring managers now search Google for information on potential candidates before making a job offer.)

Cell Phone Etiquette

How can you show respect for others and make yourself a savvy user of cell phones?

Etiquette is about presenting yourself with polish and making those around you comfortable. It is hard to find an area in more need of considerations than that of cell phone usage. See Table 5.4 for some strategies to make cell phone usage professional.

5.4 Cell Phone Strategies for Professionals

* Don't let inappropriate ringing interfere with business. Turn off your phone.

* Speak softly. Don't annoy or bother those around you.

* Turn your phone off or set it to vibrate at a dinner meeting.

* Don't think you are so important that you need to be reachable every minute.

* Use your voice mail and return calls at an appropriate time.

* Make sure your voice-mail system is working and your mailbox is not full.

Cell Phone Strategies for Professionals

✳ Ask permission before taking someone's picture with your camera phone.

✳ Don't air dirty laundry in public. Keep a civil and pleasant tone (K.D. Pagana, in press a).

How can you handle confidential information on a cell phone?

It is best to avoid discussing confidential information on a cell phone unless you are in a private area. People near you or the recipient may be able to hear your message. Be careful not to violate the privacy of another person by mentioning him or her by name.

 **X** *Faux Pas*

A woman was in her final interview for a job position. She was the top candidate until her cell phone rang. She answered the call and proceeded to discuss her dinner plans. She was not offered the position.

What should you do if your cell phone rings during an interview?

Apologize and turn off your phone without looking to see who called. People have lost jobs because they answered their phones during an interview. Remember to turn off your phone before the interview.

Is it OK to put your cell phone on a conference table at an interview or on a dinner table in a restaurant?

No. Using your cell phone is inconsiderate and intrusive in these situations.

"Be a master of your phone, not a slave to it!"

—Emily Post

What should you do if you need to be accessible by cell phone during a business meeting?

The vast majority of callers do not need immediate access to you. Of course, some exceptions would be expectant fathers and people on a transplant list or team. In these cases and in other important circumstances, alert the other people before the meeting and keep your phone on vibrate. Leave the room when you get a call.

What is the polite thing to do if you are talking on a cell phone and it is your turn to order at a service counter?

This has become a common problem. Get off your phone when it is your turn to order. For the sake of the attendant and those waiting behind you, focus only on your order. If you are in the middle of a call and your call is important, let the person behind you order before you while you finish your call.

Do you have any recommendations for talking while driving?

Talking on a cell phone while driving a car is dangerous. In some states, it is illegal to drive with a hand-held cell phone. Police departments are starting to include questions about cell phones in their accident reports. Cell-phone distraction causes more than 2,600 deaths and 330,000 injuries in the United States every year (Human Factors and Ergonomics Society, 2005). Even hands-free cell phone calls are dangerous, because the driver is still distracted.

Avoid using your phone in high-traffic areas or in tricky situations. Turn off your cell phone or let it ring. Check your voice mail when you get off the road. Pull off the road if you need to make a call while you are driving. Do not read or send a text message while driving.

When Not to Use Your Cell Phone

Here is a short list. Basically, avoid using it anywhere you can bother or distract others.

- Worship services
- Weddings and funerals
- Public restrooms
- Libraries
- Doctors' offices
- Public performances and movie theaters
- Restaurants
- Meetings
- Public transportation

Is it OK to use your phone while walking on a busy street?

Yes, but be careful and watch out for traffic. Be alert to your surroundings. If distracted by your phone, you can be an easy target for pickpockets and thieves.

How can you use your cell phone in a polite manner at airports or train stations?

It is important not to bother others, especially in enclosed areas where you trap those around you as unwilling listeners. Here are some suggestions:

* Speak softly.

* Move away from close proximity to others.

* Speak briefly.

* Don't talk just to pass the time.

* Balance the convenience of the cell phone with the inconvenience it can cause others.

* Save any nonurgent calls for later (K.D. Pagana, in press a).

Voice-Mail Etiquette

How can you make sure your voice-mail message conveys the right impression?

This is an important topic, because voice mail is a necessity for all professionals. How you use your voice mail can work for you or against you. See Table 5.5 for some guidelines to support a professional image.

5.5 Guidelines for Voice-Mail Etiquette

* Jot down your key message points before you call.

* Always be prepared to leave a message.

* Be concise and brief. Show respect for the listener's time.

* Maintain a business tone. Don't respond when angry.

* Always state the purpose of your call.

* Don't say anything confidential in a voice mail. Others may overhear your message.

* Don't leave messages from noisy restaurants or parties.

Guidelines for Voice-Mail Etiquette (continued)

✴ Know that voice mails can be forwarded to anyone.

✴ Don't play your voice-mail messages on a speakerphone.

✴ Don't use voice mail to avoid having a difficult conversation.

How can you avoid leaving a garbled message?

Enunciate clearly and speak slowly. Instead of saying "50," which can sound like "15," say "five zero." Any number ending in "teen" can be confusing. State these numbers clearly. If possible, listen to your message. Many voice-mail systems let you listen to your message, erase it, and start over. Take advantage of this functionality whenever possible. This is particularly relevant if you tend to pepper your messages with "ahs" or "ums."

TIP

When you say your phone number, write it in the air or on a piece of paper. This will slow you down and give the person time to write it down.

How can you sound confident when leaving a message?

Stand up and smile when you leave your message. Your voice sounds more confident when you are standing. Also, the listener can hear the smile in your voice.

Is it appropriate to mention a good time for the person to call you back?

Yes, this helps avoid telephone tag. People appreciate getting this information.

If the person already has your phone number, should you leave it on a voice mail?

Yes. Leave your full name and phone number. It is more convenient for the person, and he or she will not have to look it up. Say your name and phone number at the beginning and end of your message. Or, say them twice at the end, so the recipient does not need to re-play your message.

How can you optimize your own voice-mail message system?

Here are some tips to make sure your system is running well and will support a professional image:

* Check the greeting message on your machine. Revise the greeting if it sounds unprofessional or if you hear distracting noises in the background.

* Test your system to make sure it is working. Having your phone ring indefinitely or having callers hear that your mail-box is full is unprofessional.

* Check your messages frequently so you can respond to all messages within 24 hours.

* Update your greeting message after a vacation or out-of-office period.

* Listen to all your messages before responding. A later message may negate the need to return a call (K.D. Pagana, 2007d; K.D. Pagana, 2008).

Fax Machine Courtesy

How can you extend your courtesy to people on the receiving end of your fax transmissions?

A key consideration is not to send unsolicited faxes. Many people view them as worse than junk mail, because they waste paper and tie up the machine. See Table 5.6 for some tips to guide you when you send faxes.

(5.6) Tips for Sending Faxes

* Obtain permission before sending the fax.

* Always use a cover sheet and include the number of pages. This will alert the recipient if only a portion of the fax comes through.

* If the recipient uses a shared fax machine, call and let him or her know when you send a fax.

* If the message is more than a few pages, use another option for delivery, such as overnight or express mail.

* When composing a fax, use a slightly larger font so your message is easier to read.

* Consider the hour of the night or morning that a fax is sent, especially when dealing with a home office.

What should be included in a fax cover sheet?

The cover sheet should contain the name, address, phone number, and fax number of the sender and the recipient. It also needs the date, number of pages sent (including the cover sheet), and any pertinent messages. If delivery is urgent, that should be written on the cover sheet.

Frequently Asked Questions

(?) Does call waiting have a place in business?

Only use it if you are expecting an important call, and you have told your caller ahead of time. Otherwise, do not use it during a professional call. Using call waiting implies the unknown caller is more important than the person you are speaking with at the time. Ignore the clicks.

(?) May I use emoticons in professional correspondence?

These bouncy smiley faces are OK in personal e-mails, but don't use them in a business setting.

(?) Can I use just the subject line for a short e-mail?

Yes. As an example, you could say, "Can we meet for lunch? Then finish the sentence with "EOM," the acronym for "end of message" (Whitmore, 2005).

(?) Is it OK to leave an important message on a voice-mail machine?

Yes, but only if you follow up to make sure the message was received.

(?) Can people tell if I put them on my speakerphone?

Yes. The echo of a speakerphone is easily identifiable. You need to ask permission before putting anyone on a speakerphone.

(?) What do you think of people who begin a phone conversation by saying, "How are you today?"

Don't begin your call this way. You will sound like a telemarketer. Start by identifying yourself.

If I called someone and we are disconnected, who is responsible for calling back?

You are. Since you placed the call, you know how to reach the person. The person may not know how to reach you.

TAKE-AWAY TIPS

✓ Smile when you use the phone.

✓ Schedule telephone appointments for important calls.

✓ Use speakerphones for conference calls only.

✓ Don't read or send a text message while driving your car.

✓ Your e-mail is a reflection of your professionalism or lack of it.

✓ Keep your personal e-mails out of the workplace.

✓ Ask permission before taking someone's picture with your camera phone.

6

*

Mingling Amongst the Cocktail Set

Juggling Drinks and Hors d'Oeuvres at Corporate Events

Do you:

Feel anxious and wonder if you should attend the holiday party at all?

Know what to wear?

Know how to initiate and sustain small talk?

Know how much you can drink and still be appropriate?

Know how to handle drinks and hors d'oeuvres?

Wonder if you should bring a gift?

Have a spouse who does not want to attend your business function?

Wonder if you should send a thank-you note afterward?

These are important concerns for new and even seasoned employees. Inappropriate behavior at cocktail parties and corporate events can undo years of good impressions. Your career aspirations can be enhanced or limited by your behavior as you navigate these potentially disastrous social gatherings.

"Etiquette is what you are doing and saying when people are looking and listening. What you are thinking is your business."

—Virginia Cary Hudson

Greetings and Courtesies

Is it really necessary to attend your office party?

Yes, unless you want to be remembered as the person who snubbed your colleagues by not attending. Your absence at an annual function will be noted.

Attending the party shows you are a team player and gives you a chance to get to know co-workers in a less formal setting. Think of the office party as part of your job. If this is not your idea of a good time, consider it work. Put on your best attitude and go. If you are unable to attend, let your host and others know why.

What should you do if you have accepted an invitation and discover at the last minute that you cannot attend?

Make every effort to contact the host. Here are some other suggestions:

* Call to the location of the event and leave a message with the banquet manager or maître d' to be passed to the host.

* Send a handwritten note the next day explaining your absence.

* Call the host the next day. Apologize and explain your situation (Rickenbacher, 2004).

Is a business party a time to relax and "let loose"?

No. It is a test of your social skills and your level of sophistication. Your interpersonal skills, including your treatment of the wait staff, are on display. One of the biggest blunders at a business function is alcohol abuse. You can undo months and years of good impressions by excessive drinking. The key point to remember is that "business" is the number one concern at the gathering (K.D. Pagana, 2006c).

Why are many people uncomfortable attending social events?

Fewer people are raised with "social graces" as a priority in their lives. Teenagers and children have unprecedented time demands from school and extracurricular activities, and in most families, both parents work full-time jobs. This means that fewer people have time to focus on learning social graces—including "small talk"—and contributes to the anxiety that many people feel in formal or business functions.

For many people, including nurses on the job, time is so precious that we practice getting to the point and the task at hand as quickly as possible, so we can move on to the next point or task. However, many businesses expect employees to have the social skills that will make them a competent representative for the organization.

No matter your age, social skills are important for career advancement. Learn them! In addition to this book, there are numerous resources available. Many community, business, and school organizations offer courses that teach these skills.

✗ Faux Pas

Bill was being honored at a cocktail party for receiving a national award. His family members were invited. His sisters stuck together and made no effort to interact with anyone else. Unfortunately, they lost the opportunity to meet Bill's colleagues. They could have asked, "How do you know Bill?" as a conversation starter and met a lot of nice people. Instead, they came across as backward and socially awkward. They were not an asset to Bill in his goal for career advancement.

When should I arrive for a company party?

It is best to arrive on time. Do not be more than 15-20 minutes late (Post & Post, 1999). A late entrance will make people think you are rude. Punctuality is expected more at a business event than a social event.

✓ Good Idea!

As the new VP of nursing, Felix was looking forward to getting to know the administrative team better at the board retreat. As part of his preparation for the weekend, he found out as much as he could about the people who were going to be there. Because of this preparation, he had no trouble fitting in with the team as he used small talk to initiate conversations and begin to develop working relationships.

Don't arrive early. This can be awkward for the host if he or she is not quite ready for the party and feels the need to talk to you.

Do you recommend bringing family or a partner to a business event?

If they are invited and you would like them to attend, that is fine. Just be aware that their actions and dress will reflect on you. You should brief them ahead of time on proper dress, conversational topics, key people, and expected behavior.

Do you have any recommendations for presenting oneself professionally at a corporate event?

Think of this as a great opportunity to expand your network and make new friends. This is where you can practice your skills related to introductions, handshaking, remembering names, conversations, and networking. See Table 6.1 for some guidelines.

 Presenting Oneself Professionally

✻ Smile and be friendly to everyone.

✻ Avoid clustering in small groups with people in your department.

✻ Introduce yourself to people you don't know.

✻ Take the time and effort to get acquainted with new people.

✻ Spend more time listening than talking.

✻ Ask open-ended questions.

✻ Keep the conversational topics accessible to everyone.

✻ Minimize "shop talk" during social gatherings.

✻ Be sure to greet senior management. Use engaging small talk.

✻ If you don't call people by their first names at work, don't start at the social event.

✻ Don't take or make any phone calls.

✻ Treat the servers with respect.

✻ Don't act bored. Be aware of your body language.

✻ Time your departure. Don't be the first or the last person to leave.

✻ Thank your hosts before leaving.

(Brody, 2005; Pachter, 2006a; Sabath, 2002).

Why is small talk important at a corporate function?

Small talk is essential for starting conversations until you find a common area of interest. It is a valuable tool for breaking the ice and making people feel comfortable. Small talk is a gateway to new relationships and vital for maintaining established relationships.

If you have trouble getting started with small talk, try using the OAR approach to help your conversation.

* **O**bserve. Make an observation. (For example, "It looks like this new restaurant drew a large crowd.")

* **A**sk questions. (For example, "How is your daughter doing on the swim team?")

* **R**eveal something about yourself. (For example, "Now that I've been at Susquehanna Health for 3 years, it is nice to know most of the people here.")

How do you know what topics are safe for conversation?

Avoid controversial topics, especially religion and politics. Don't discuss salary, medical problems, or personal misfortunes. You can safely discuss weather, sports, traffic, travel, movies, and books. Avoid off-color jokes.

During a social event, don't discuss work problems. Avoid medical jargon. If a conversation turns to work, change the subject by saying something like: "I heard you mention a trip earlier. Where are you planning to go?"

Don't forget to protect patient privacy in your conversations. It is unethical and illegal to discuss patients outside of the health care team.

X *Faux Pas*

Joe invited his friend Patrick to play golf with him and two of his colleagues in the fundraiser for the new cancer treatment center. Although Patrick was a good golfer, Joe regretted inviting him to the tournament because Patrick talked the entire time about his medical problems. He dominated the conversation and put a damper on the golf outing.

How do you exit gracefully from conversations?

This is a key component of networking at corporate events. Your goal is to meet several people and not spend the entire time speaking with one person. Simply excuse yourself and say something like: "It has been great talking with you. I'll let you have time to speak to others." Or, "It was a pleasure meeting you. Will you excuse me while I touch base with some other colleagues?"

✓ Good Idea!

Theresa was attending her first corporate cocktail party. She didn't want to make a bad impression by heading straight to the buffet to get something to eat, so she ate something before she arrived. Once there, she ordered a soda with a lime, which she carried in her left hand, leaving her right hand free to shake hands. She met many new people and had a great time at the party. She was very savvy and conducted herself with charm, which her managers noticed. When she got home, she and her husband shared a bottle of wine and discussed the party.

What is the dress code for a corporate event?

The key word here is "corporate." Make sure you dress appropriately for the function by checking the invitation or making a phone call to the host. Remember: The way you dress when out with friends and family may not be suitable for a work function. Take time to dress up. It is always best to err on the more formal side. Your effort will be apparent and reflect favorably on you.

TIP

Women should avoid clothes that are too tight, too short, and too sexy.

How do you deal with gossip?

Avoid gossipers. It is not enough to abstain from gossip. Silence can be a form of participation. Excuse yourself and remove yourself from the situation.

If there are no place cards on the dinner tables, can you sit wherever you want?

Yes. But, be sure you are not sitting at the host's table. If people are already seated at a table, ask them for permission to join their table. As an example, you may say: "Do you mind if I join you?" or "Are these chairs available?" A chair tilted against the table means that place is taken.

If I am invited to a party at someone's house, should I bring a gift?

Yes. The host expends a lot of time and money to put on a party. A small gift expresses your appreciation and gratitude. The gift does not have to be expensive, but it should be nicely wrapped. Some suggestions include a bottle of wine, fragrant candles, or a box of chocolates. Small gift baskets with jams or gourmet foods are also a nice option. Attach a card so the host will know who brought it. If you bring wine, do not expect the host to serve it at the party. If you bring flowers, put them in a vase before giving them to the host.

Should I send a thank-you note after the occasion?

Yes, if you want to show appreciation, demonstrate good manners, and be remembered. This should be a handwritten note.

"Always do sober what you said you'd do drunk. That will teach you to keep your mouth shut."

—Ernest Hemingway

Alcoholic Beverages and Hors d'Oeuvres

Do you have any suggestions for drinking at a corporate event?

Limit yourself to one or two drinks. This can be a challenge when the drinks are free and the liquor is high quality. Don't think you need to drink to be part of the group. Stop drinking when you reach your limit, and switch to a nonalcoholic beverage. You do not want to be remembered for any colorful or inappropriate behavior. You will be held accountable for your actions.

If you are at a ballgame with your boss and colleagues, is it OK to drink?

Yes, if you can handle yourself in an appropriate manner. Remember that your behavior at the ballgame will be remembered in the boardroom.

TIP

Business is the number one item on the agenda at any business event.

What is the best way to hold drinks and hors d'oeuvres?

The best way is to handle them separately. It is very awkward to hold a drink in one hand and food in the other. This restricts your ability to shake hands. Remember, the purpose of the event is to socialize, not to eat and drink. Don't be hungry and thirsty when you arrive at the event.

✗ Faux Pas

Justin was at a corporate out-of-town dinner with his team. His boss offered wine and Justin, along with the rest of the team, accepted the offer of a glass. When the wine was brought to the table, a co-worker who had been drinking before and during the meal grabbed the glass the waiter had offered to the boss to taste and approve. In addition to this behavior, she was the only one who ordered an after-dinner drink. Everyone at the table was embarrassed for her. Her career with the hospital was short-lived, as this inappropriate behavior was also demonstrated—in less dramatic ways—in her everyday work.

TIP

It is hard to be polite when you are starved. Eat something before the event.

What do you do with the toothpick used to serve food from a serving tray?

Don't put the toothpick back on the tray. Put the toothpick in your napkin or on a tray used to collect empty glasses and plates.

✗ Faux Pas

Dave made sure he was appropriately dressed for the office party at a nice country club. He limited his drinking to one glass of wine. However, he stood by the shrimp bar and ate more than 20 pieces of shrimp. He forgot that the main purpose of the event was to mingle and network. His co-workers did not forget this incident. They endlessly teased him and made him the butt of many shrimp jokes.

Avoiding Buffet Blunders

- Put your food selections on a plate.
- Don't snack over the buffet table.
- Move away from the table to eat your food.
- Don't complain about the food. Just select food you like and pass on food you do not want.
- Don't double-dip your food in sauces.

Wine Service and Drinking

What is the proper way for the host to handle wine at a meal?

See Table 6.2 for tips on handling wine if you are the host.

6.2   Wine-Handling Tips for the Host

✳ The server presents the wine bottle to the host.

✳ The host examines the label to make certain it is the correct type and vintage.

✳ The server removes the seal, takes out the cork, and places the cork on the table.

✳ The host looks at the cork to make sure it is in good condition.

✳ The server pours a small amount of wine into a glass for the host to sample.

✳ The host can swirl the wine in a small motion, sniff the wine, and take a small sip.

Wine-Handling Tips for the Host   (continued)

* If the wine tastes good, the guests are served before the host.

* If the wine tastes "off" or has a musky odor, the problem is reported to the server. The server or wine steward may taste to confirm. A replacement bottle will be provided.

Is there a different type of wine glass used for white and red wine?

Yes. A red wine glass has a short stem and a large bowl. Red wine is served at room temperature. Hold the glass close to the bowl.

A white wine glass has a longer stem and a smaller bowl. White wine is served chilled. Hold the glass by the stem to avoid warming the wine with the heat from your hand.

How much money should you spend on a bottle of wine?

A sensible guideline is to spend as much on a bottle of wine as the cost of one complete dinner. Be careful. Wine prices vary from a few dollars to hundreds of dollars.

How can you have the wine steward suggest a wine in your price range?

Point to some prices on the menu and ask for suggestions.

In which hand should you hold your glass of wine?

Keep your drink in your left hand, so your right hand is free for shaking hands. You don't want your right hand to be cold and damp.

Should you tip the bartender?

If it is a cash bar where you pay for your drinks, you should tip the bartender. At most formal affairs, gratuities are built into the wait staff's fees (Post & Post, 1999).

How do you select wine?

Red wines are usually recommended with red meats, although this rule is not carved in stone. White wines are usually recommended with white meats or fish. However, these are just suggestions. You can ask the wine steward to make suggestions to complement your meal choices.

Popular examples of red wines include merlot, zinfandel, shiraz, and pinot noir. Popular whites include chardonnay and sauvignon blanc (Pachter, 2006a).

How do you know how many bottles of wine to order for a group of people?

As a rule of thumb, consider one bottle for three people (Pachter, 2006a).

Beer Drinking

If you are drinking beer at a corporate event, should you use a glass?

Yes. Pour it into a pilsner glass. Stay away from plastic glasses unless no others are available.

Do you have any suggestions for drinking beer at a cocktail party or dinner?

Yes. Pour the beer into a large glass that will hold the entire can or bottle. This avoids the need to put beer cans or bottles on the table. At a formal party, it looks classier to carry a glass of beer instead of a bottle or can. However, if you are at a function where the hosts are drinking from a bottle or can, feel free to do the same. If you have a question about how to handle a drink or food, follow the lead of your host or those in the position you aspire to.

Tasteful Toasting

The custom of wine toasting to health dates back to ancient Greece, when a sip was taken to demonstrate that the wine was not poisoned. Splashing wine from cup to cup was also a safeguard against poisoning. Today, a toast is used to recognize a special occasion (Whitmore, 2005).

How can you make a memorable toast?

Keep it simple and short. It is a toast, not a roast. Prepare ahead of time so you do not fumble for the appropriate words.

Can anyone propose the first toast at an event?

The host or hostess should propose the first toast. If there is a guest of honor, the host or hostess should toast the person. The honored guest should respond with a toast. Other guests are then free to make toasts.

If the guest of honor is being toasted, does he or she take a drink?

No. The person being honored should smile and say thank you. It is considered bad form to drink to oneself.

If you do not drink alcohol, can you participate in the toast?

Yes. You can toast with a nonalcoholic beverage or water. You can also raise a glass of wine to your lips without tasting it.

Are there any toasting blunders to avoid?

Yes. Here are some tips to prevent blunders:

* Do not read a toast. However, you may glance at your written speech.

* Don't clink glasses.

* Do not tap the rim of a glass to get everyone's attention.

* Don't toast yourself.

* You do not need to drink alcohol to propose a toast.

* Don't raise your glass above eye level.

Frequently Asked Questions

 Should I stand up if the host stands to make a toast to someone?

Yes. However, the person being toasted should remain seated.

Is it OK to rearrange the place cards at a table?

No. Sit where the host wanted you to sit.

 How soon should I respond to an RSVP?

It is best to respond within a few days to a week. But, most definitely respond before the date indicated. The RSVP means you have to respond one way or another. Don't make the host have to call you for your response. If you decline, include a brief reason for your regret.

 When is an RSVP unnecessary?

Invitations without an RSVP do not require them. For many of these events, the invitation may indicate "regrets only" as a way of getting a head count. In this case, you respond only if you are *not* planning to attend. Otherwise your attendance is expected.

 If you meet someone at an event and suggest having lunch, what is the appropriate follow-up?

Don't suggest lunch unless you mean it. Be sure to follow up with a phone call or note within a few days.

 How much do you tip a bartender?

The usual is $1 per drink at the bar.

 When should a guest leave an event?

It is polite to leave at or before the ending time for the event. Don't overstay your welcome. If you are having a good time, keep track of the time. If the invitation said 5-7 p.m., don't stay a minute after 7 p.m.

What should I do if I end up with something in my mouth that I don't like or can't chew?

Transfer it to your cocktail napkin, and then place the napkin in a trashcan or on a service tray for collecting used plates and glasses.

TAKE-AWAY TIPS

✓ Loose lips sink ships, so be careful to keep your conversation within appropriate parameters. Don't say anything to anyone that you will be embarrassed about later or that could get you into professional trouble.

✓ Be discreet with your conversation. Avoid divulging your personal troubles.

✓ Avoid foods that can get messy. Keep your hands clean for handshakes.

✓ You can be sociable and not drink alcohol.

✓ Respond promptly to all invitations.

✓ If someone is toasting you, do not drink to yourself.

✓ Business rules apply even in business social settings.

✓ If in doubt, don't. For instance, if you question whether you should wear something, don't.

7

✳

How Dining Etiquette and Business Success Go Hand-in-Hand

Seeing Through That Silverware Glare

Do you:

Know which water glass is yours?

Know which fork to use first?

Know what to do if you drop your fork under the table?

Know what to do if you need to blow your nose at a meal?

Know what to do if someone asks you a question and your mouth is full?

These are concerns that can make you feel flustered or uncomfortable during a meal. The fast-food world and the school cafeteria do not provide many opportunities for learning the finer points of dining etiquette. However, minding your manners can make a lasting impression in a business or formal setting. Read on for guidelines to make you feel more comfortable and confident while dining during business meetings, job interviews, wedding receptions, or other special occasions.

X *Faux Pas*

Sean had just finished his master's degree. He was invited to a business lunch as part of the interview process. Sean overheard the person to his right asking the wait staff for a fork. He realized then that he was using the fork belonging to that person. He was embarrassed and worried about other etiquette blunders he may have committed.

Place Settings

Where is your bread plate?

One of the challenges of dining with others is figuring out which bread plate belongs to you and which water glass is yours. However, there are several mnemonic devices that make it easy to remember your way around a formal dinner table.

* All food to the left of the entrée plate belongs to you. This includes your salad, bread, and soup. ("Food" and "left" both have four letters.)

* All drinks to the right of the entrée plate are yours. This includes your water, wine, and coffee cup. ("Drink" and "right" both have five letters.)

* "Fork" has four letters and is placed to the left (four letters) of the plate. "Knife" and "spoon," both with five letters, are placed on the right (five letters) of the plate.

* If you can remember the expression "*left*-over bread," you can remember that your bread is on the left.

* Another easy way is remember proper table setting positioning is to think of a **BMW** car and think "**B**read, **M**eal, and **W**ater." Your bread is on the left, your meal is in the center, and your water glass is on the right. (K.D. Pagana, 2006b).

Your bread, meal, and water appear in this order from left to right, just like the letters of a BMW automobile.

Bread and Butter

Who should pass the bread around?

If the bread is in a basket in front of you, pick it up and offer it to the person to your left. Then, take a piece yourself and pass it to your right. Or, you can just pick it up and pass it to your right (counterclockwise).

If someone already started passing the bread the wrong way, just go with it. Also, remember, once you touch a piece of bread, it is yours. Definitely do not reach into the basket and feel for a hot roll on the bottom.

Do not serve yourself first.

How much bread can you butter?

If the butter is being passed around, put a pat of butter on your bread plate. When eating the bread, tear off a piece. Then butter and eat one piece at a time. Some restaurants feature special oil for bread. If so, pour or spoon out a small amount onto your bread plate. NEVER dip your bread into the community oil.

Soup

How do you handle the soup?

Many meals start with soup, which can be a challenge.

* When eating soup, dip the spoon sideways into the soup toward the back of the bowl—away from you. This technique prevents the soup from splashing onto your clothes.

* Skim the top of the soup with the spoon and sip from the side of your spoon, not from the front.

* Don't crumble crackers into the soup. Take one bite at a time, just like with bread.

* You can tilt the bowl away from you to get the soup from the bottom of the bowl. If the soup bowl has two handles, you can pick it up and drink from the bowl. However, this method is not widely known or commonly done.

* If the soup is hot, don't blow on it. Just wait until it cools down a bit. When finished, place your spoon next to the bowl on the plate. If there is no plate, leave the spoon in the bowl.

If the meal is during an important meeting for work, it's best to just avoid soups that are messy and hard to eat. Even if you love French onion soup, don't order it at a business meal. If it is pre-ordered, use your spoon to break the cheese against the back of the bowl so you are not stretching strings of cheese from the bowl to your mouth.

"At a dinner party, one should eat wisely but not too well, and talk well but not too wisely."

—W. Somerset Maugham

Dining Utensils

Which fork should I use first?

* Work from outside to inside.

* The salad fork will be the smaller fork on the outside, and the larger dinner fork will be on the inside.

* Used utensils do not go back on the tablecloth. They are placed on the salad or entrée plate.

X *Faux Pas*

As an acknowledgement of her Award for Clinical Excellence, Lindsey was being honored at a banquet attended by the medical center administration. She was so overwhelmed and confused by the many pieces of silverware, china, and glasses that she could not enjoy the meal or the conversation. She worried the entire time about making an etiquette blunder and leaving a bad impression on the administrators.

Salads

Can I cut the salad?

Sure you can. Most salads do not have bite-size pieces of lettuce. Therefore, use your knife and fork to cut the salad.

✓ *Good Idea!*

Jennifer placed a copy of *The Nurses's Etiquette Advantage* in the hospital breakroom. As the nurses were relaxing, they started asking each other questions from the book. They quickly realized that there was a lot of information they could learn before the upcoming holiday dinner. Several of the nurses purchased copies of the book for stocking stuffers.

* Be careful handling cherry tomatoes. Use one of the tines of your fork to poke into the stem area of the tomato. This will prevent the cherry tomato from shooting across the table when you cut it.

* If your salad has olives with pits, the pits are removed from your mouth with your fork and placed on the edge of your salad plate.

* If the salad dressing is in front of you, pick it up, offer it to the person on your left, serve your-self, and pass to your right. Or, just pick it up and pass it to your right.

American and Continental Dining Styles

How many pieces of meat may I cut at a time?

This answer depends on whether you follow the American or Continental/European style of dining. Although both are acceptable in

the United States, the American style is most commonly used. The
Continental/European style is the norm outside of the United States.

* American style is sometimes called the "zig-zag" style, because
  the meat is cut with the knife in the right hand and fork in the
  left. (The opposite hands are used for a left-handed person.)
  Two or three pieces of meat are cut. Then, the fork is switched
  to the right hand to eat the meat. The knife is placed across
  the top of the plate with the blade pointing inward.

* Continental style places the knife in the right hand and the
  fork in the left hand. Each piece of meat is consumed as it is
  cut. The silverware is not shifted around to the other hand.

Is there a way to signal to the wait staff when you are finished with your plate?

Yes. You signal the wait staff by positioning your silverware on your
plate to indicate the resting and finished positions. These positions
help you keep pace with your dinner partners.

* The resting position allows you to slow down and keeps your
  plate on the table. This is particularly useful if you are a fast
  eater. Removal of your plate from the table puts pressure on
  others to speed up.

* The finish position signals the wait staff that the plate can be
  removed (K.D. Pagana, 2006a).

American Style:

Imagine a clock on your plate. To indicate that you are resting and
do not want your plate removed, place the fork with its top pointed
at 10 o'clock and the base at the 4 o'clock position. The knife is
placed across the top of the plate with the blade pointed inward.

To indicate that you are finished, place the knife and fork in the 10 and 4 o'clock position with the tops of the silverware pointed at 10 and the bottoms pointed at 4.

American: Rest

American: Finish

Continental Style:

To indicate a resting position, the fork and knife are placed in an inverted "V" position. To indicate that you are finished, place the knife and fork in the 10 and 4 o'clock position with the tops of the silverware pointed at 10 and the bottoms pointed at 4. This is the same as the American style.

Continental: Rest

Continental: Finish

Napkin Placement

Where do I put the napkin?

When everyone sits down at the table, napkins are placed on the lap. If you need to excuse yourself during the meal, place the napkin on your chair so others do not see your soiled napkin on the table.

X *Faux Pas*

A group of co-workers were eating dinner at an upscale restaurant. One man pulled out some dental floss and flossed his teeth at the table. This uncouth behavior ruined the appetites of everyone else at the table.

When the meal is finished and everyone is leaving the table, put the napkin to the left of the plate. If the plate is already removed, put the napkin where the plate was (K.D. Pagana, 2006c).

X *Faux Pas*

In her new position as vice president of nursing, Veronica was invited to a corporate dinner at an exclusive private dining club with the members of the board of trustees. She was served an exquisite meal by a doting wait staff. During the meal, she was asked a question and she put her silverware on her plate. With an attentive wait staff, someone was there in a flash to whisk away her plate. Unfortunately, Veronica had placed her silverware in the finish position. She was stunned, and her facial expression gave away her surprise to her dinner partner, who was gracious enough to discretely alert Veronica to the importance of handling silverware appropriately during a formal dinner. Veronica decided then and there to learn as much about dining etiquette as she could before the next dinner party.

Table Manners Dos and Don'ts

Do:

Say "please" and "thank you."

Chew with your mouth closed.

Pass the salt and pepper together.

Place the salt and pepper shakers on the table in front of the person requesting them.

Taste your food before seasoning.

Wait for others to be served before starting to eat.

Encourage others to start eating if your food is held up.

Say "excuse me" if you have to go to the restroom during dinner.

Don't:

Put your elbows on the table.

Re-arrange the place cards on the table.

Wave your utensils.

Slurp your soup.

Pick your teeth.

Blow your nose on the dinner napkin.

Put on lipstick or make-up.

Comb your hair.

Ask for a doggie bag at a business meal or buffet.

Say, "I have to go to the bathroom."

Paying the Bill

Who pays the bill?

The host should pay the bill and leave the tip. (Be prepared in case the host does not know this.) The host should be able to figure out the tip without using a calculator. Good service usually is acknowledged with a 15-20% tip. If everyone will be paying separately, alert the waiter before ordering to let him or her know to provide separate checks.

X Faux Pas

Colleen and four of her co-workers were invited to dinner by their manager to celebrate the completion of a successful project. Colleen ordered a soup and salad. The manager ordered prime rib. When the waiter gave the bill to the manager, he divided it by six and told everyone to pay an equal share of the bill. The manager's inconsiderate decision was upsetting for Colleen, because she only ordered what she knew she could afford. Since the manager invited Colleen and her co-workers out to dinner, he should have paid the bill.

For a shared check, be sure to have cash on hand to pay for everything you ordered, including tax and tip. If everyone ordered the same thing, divide the check after adding the tip.

Tips for Buffets

* Wait for the serving staff or host to direct your table to the buffet.

* Don't overload your plate. You can always go back after everyone has gotten food.

* Don't leave the serving spoon or fork in the serving dish. Place it on the saucer in front of the serving dish. This will prevent the handle from sliding into the dish.

* If you are the first one back to the table with food, wait for at least one other person to join you before you start to eat.

✓ Good Idea!

Amy was planning to take her father and stepmother out for dinner to celebrate her father's birthday. Two days before the dinner, she called to verify the reservation. While on the phone, she found out that the restaurant accepted only cash as payment. She had been unaware of this policy before calling to confirm the reservation. Amy now asks about payment policies when she makes reservations.

* Use a new plate when you return to the buffet.

* Don't ask for a doggie bag.

 **X** *Faux Pas*

Barb and her husband went out to dinner with Denise, a work colleague, and her husband. While Barb was squeezing a lemon, the juice squirted across the table into Denise's eyes. The discomfort was significant for Denise, and it was several minutes before the group could continue the meal. Barb was mortified. After that, she wasted no time in learning how to handle difficult meal situations such as squeezing lemons.

Tips for Handling Difficult Foods

Do you have any recommendations for handling difficult foods in a formal setting?

Yes. Don't order them at a formal setting. Save them for eating at home or with friends in an informal setting. Here are some tips for some challenging foods.

* *Bacon*: Use a fork. However, if the bacon is crisp, you may pick it up with your fingers.

* *Bananas*: Peel, cut into slices, and eat with a fork.

* *Cherries with pits*: Use a spoon to put the cherry into your mouth and to remove the pit from your mouth.

* *Corn on the cob*: Butter a few rows at a time. Hold with both hands.

* *French fries*: Cut into bite-size pieces and eat with a fork.

* *Lemons*: Cup in your hand to avoid squirting as you squeeze it over food or into drinks.

* *Parfait*: Start at the top and inch your way down.

* *Pasta*: Use your fork to twirl a few strands against the edge of your plate. (In less formal settings, you can use a spoon for twirling.)

* *Petits fours*: These are finger foods that are eaten in small bites.

* *Pork chops*: Use a knife and fork.

* *Cherry tomatoes*: Use the tine of the fork to poke into the area where the stem was attached. Cut into pieces.

* *Watermelon*: Use a knife and fork. Use a spoon if watermelon is shaped into small balls (K.D. Pagana, 2006b).

 Good Idea!

In her position as vice president, Candace often hosts meals for male and female colleagues. To avoid an uncomfortable moment when the dinner check arrives, Candace gives the maitre d' her credit card ahead of time and asks to have an 18% tip added. After the meal, she is presented the bill and merely has to sign it. She tells everyone that they are guests of the organization.

Frequently Asked Questions

(?) May I turn over my coffee cup to indicate that I do not want coffee?

No, never turn over any plate, cup, or wine glass.

Should I tell a dinner partner if he or she has food in his or her teeth?

Yes, people want to know this.

 Where should women place their purses?

If the purse is small, it can go on the lap under the napkin. If it's a large purse, she should put it on the floor between her feet or by her right foot, with the plan to exit the seat by the right side. Purses should not be placed on the backs of chairs. They can be in the way of the servers and get stolen easily.

 What should I do if I get a fish bone in my mouth?

Use your fingers to remove fish bones. Place them on the edge of your plate.

 What if I have food in my mouth when someone asks me a question?

Point to your mouth and the questioner will get the hint. To take the pressure off you, he or she should ask someone else a question so everyone isn't looking at you and waiting for you to answer the question.

 May I dip my bread into the sauce on my plate?

Tear off a piece of bread and put it on your plate. Use your fork to spear the bread, dip it into the sauce, and eat it.

 May I tuck the napkin into my collar?

No. However, you may lift your napkin up and cover your shirt for a few seconds when eating something messy. Men should not swing their tie around to the back of their neck.

② What should I do if I drop my fork under the table?

Leave it there so you are not disappearing under the table during the meal. Ask the wait staff for another fork.

② What foods should not be ordered at a business meal?

Avoid anything you do not know how to eat and anything messy. Examples of messy foods include spaghetti, barbecue ribs, and French onion soup. Eat messy foods on your own time and with your family and friends.

② Is it polite for the meal guest to offer to pay the tip?

No, because the guest would have to know the cost of the meal to calculate the tip.

② Are there any conversational topics to avoid during a meal?

Yes! Avoid discussing religion, politics, health problems, and anything inappropriate.

② How do you get a piece of meat gristle out of your mouth?

Most etiquette experts advise removing something from your mouth with the same utensils used to put it into your mouth. In this case, that would mean using your fork. However, many people do not feel comfortable doing this and remove the meat with one hand while using the napkin to block their mouth and dab their face with the other hand. Place the meat on the rim of your plate, preferably under a piece of garnish.

TAKE-AWAY TIPS

✓ If you are trying to decide how much you can spend on your meal, ask your host for food recommendations. If the host says he or she will be getting filet mignon, you can feel free to order it also. Without any recommendations or suggestions, stay in the middle price range.

✓ When you sit at the table, enter your seat from the left and exit from the right. This is especially important at a round table when eight or 10 people are entering and exiting their chairs.

✓ Food is delivered to the table on your left side and removed from your right side. An easy way to remember this is the two "R's"— "remove" from the "right."

✓ Follow the lead of the host. If he or she passes on dessert or coffee, you should too.

8

✳

Thank-You Notes and Business Letters

How Expressing Gratitude Can Make an Impact

Do you:

Wonder if it is proper to send a thank-you note by e-mail?

Know the proper way to format a business letter?

Know thank-you notes are important but wonder when to send them?

Know the recipient's title, spelling of name, and so on?

Know to whom the letter should be addressed?

Your written words are going to leave an impression. Your challenge is to make this a positive impression, because the written word has permanence and creates a paper trail. Many people are great communicators in face-to-face contact, but they are befuddled when they have to write a letter or note.

✓ *Good Idea!*

Three different administrators interviewed Jacqueline for a new position. During each interview, she noted how each person's office was decorated. One office had golf photos, another had small statues of frogs, and the third had pictures of flowers. After the interview, she went to the mall and got cards featuring golfers, frogs, and flowers. She got the competitive edge by tailoring the cards to fit the personalities of the interviewers.

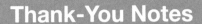
Thank-You Notes

If you thank someone for something, is it really necessary to send a thank-you note?

Yes, if you want to demonstrate good manners, show appreciation, and be remembered. A thank-you note is the 5-minute difference between *feeling grateful* and *showing your gratitude* (Spade, 2004).

> "*Gratitude is the most exquisite form of courtesy.*"
> —Jacques Maritain

Should the thank-you note be typed or handwritten?

If you are thanking someone for a gift or an event, it should be handwritten. Two or three sentences are all that is needed. Make sure you refer to the gift or the event.

If you are sending a note after an interview, the note can be handwritten or typed, depending on its length. If you want to write more than several sentences, two typed paragraphs are acceptable. Try to mention one thing you had in common with the interviewer—for example, you both worked in New York earlier in your careers.

X Faux Pas

When her son graduated from high school, Eileen had a big party for him. A week after the party, the guests received a typed thank-you note addressed to family, neighbors, and friends. It was unsigned and the names on the envelope were written in Eileen's handwriting. It was obvious that Eileen had done everything. She missed an important opportunity to teach her son important manners.

> "An engraved or printed thank-you card, no matter how attractive its design, cannot take the place of a personally written message of thanks."
>
> —Emily Post

TIP

If you type a thank-you note, be sure to sign your name.

When should you send a thank-you note?

All etiquette books agree that the sooner the better. For maximum impact, send the note within 24 hours. Ideally, you should send the note within 1 to 3 days of receiving a gift or attending an event.

✓ Good Idea!

Mark had four interviews scheduled the week before his graduation. Before the interviews, he purchased some fine quality thank-you cards. After each interview, he requested a business card. He wrote his thank-you cards in the evening after each interview and mailed them the next day. He made a good impression and had no trouble getting a position.

What if you forget to send a thank-you note and remember several weeks later?

Send the note. It is better late than never.

Examples of Thank-You Notes

Dear Theresa,

We had a wonderful time at your dinner party. The food was delicious and the company was most enjoyable. Thanks for inviting us.

> Sincerely,
> Jocelyn & Justin Balon

Dear Denise,

Christine and I enjoyed the holiday dinner party at your home. It was fun to be with so many nice people and share a delicious meal. Thank you very much.

> Happy Holidays!
> Ryan Flanery

8.1   Thank-You Note Etiquette Tips

* If you receive a gift or check, do not use the gift or cash the check until after you write the thank-you note.

* Thank the person for the specific gift and mention the gift by name. If the gift was money, don't mention the amount in your note. It is sufficient to say, "your generous gift."

* Tell the person how the gift was or will be used.

* Send a thank-you note within a few days after receiving a gift or attending an event. If possible, do it within 24 hours.

* If you forget to send a thank-you note, go ahead and send it, even if it is several months late.

* Keep quality note cards on hand for writing thank-you notes.

 Good Idea!

Tim and his family were having dinner at a restaurant. Tim saw a friend there and arranged to secretly pay for his dinner. The next day, Tim received a thank-you note in the mail. The recipient had mailed the thank-you note at the post office the evening after the dinner. Tim could not believe he received the note so quickly and was impressed with his friend's manners.

Can I e-mail a thank-you note?

Only e-mail a thank-you note if you are following it with a mailed note. Thank-you notes received after interviews are usually placed in an application file. When the applications are reviewed, a note on nice paper will reflect better on your manners than an e-mail.

Many people tack a thank-you note to a corkboard. E-mails do not have the same impact because they require only a few seconds of time and effort.

Do you have any suggestions for sending thank-you notes internationally after receiving a gift or having a phone interview?

Yes, send the note as soon as possible after the interview, event, gift, or visit. Use quality stationery. Type or print the letter to avoid mistranslation due to handwriting idiosyncrasies. (While attractive, handwriting flourishes can be confusing for someone for whom English is a second or third language.) Make sure you have the correct spelling of the person's name, and include his or her title. Check correspondence you have received from the person to verify this information. Print or type the address in the proper format for the designated country. Take the letter to the post office so it can be mailed with the proper postage and "airmail" designation.

Business Letters

Are business letters being replaced by e-mail?

No. Business letters are now often sent as an attachment to e-mail. But, note that this does not give the same impression as receiving a signed letter on good quality paper.

What are the key components of a business letter?

Letters need:

* Date
* Titles
* Addresses of sender and recipient
* Salutation
* Body or content
* Closing
* Signature

The body of the letter should be clear and succinct with a focus on "what's in it for them." Here are some helpful tips (Post & Post, 1999):

* Keep it simple.

* Be clear. Avoid jargon.

* Use active voice. ("Javier will contact the job candidate" rather than "The job candidate will be contacted by Javier." The active voice adds strength and brevity to your sentence structure.

* Avoid using run-on or incomplete sentences.

* Vary sentence structure.

* Use paragraphs. Paragraphs should not be more than four or five sentences or about seven to nine lines. Double space between paragraphs for easier reading.

* End your message. (For example, "I look forward to meeting you." Or, "Thank you for your time and consideration.")

* Use a close, such as "Sincerely," "Sincerely yours," "Best regards," or "Cordially."

* When you are enclosing materials with your letter, use "Enclosure," "enc," or "encl."

* If you are distributing your letter to others, indicate courtesy copies by "cc" or "copies to." The names of the recipients are listed alphabetically.

8.2 Common Mistakes With Business Letters

MISTAKES	*TIPS*
Misspelling the recipient's name or title	Call the secretary or check the Web site.
Having typos in the letter	Use spell check and have someone else proofread your letter.
Using an informal tone	Keep the tone formal, even if you know the recipient. Others on a committee may see the letter.
Forgetting to sign your letter	Check to make sure you signed the letter, so you do not look lazy and unprofessional.
Forgetting an attachment	If you say you are including something, make sure you add it before sealing the letter.

What are some tips for minimizing frustration and re-writing?

Organize your thoughts before you begin writing. Decide what you want to say and what you want as the outcome of your communication. Write a rough draft.

How can you avoid misspellings in a business letter?

Use your spell check. But remember, misspelled words can be overlooked by spell check when the misspelled word is a homonym—like "berth" or "birth," "capitol" or "capital," and "stationary" or "stationery"—but also misspelled words that are real words like "fist" instead of "first" or "bank" instead of "blank." Read your letter out loud. Have someone else read it for typos and misspellings. See Table 8.3 for some common misspellings in a business letter.

Sample Business Letter

23 Hawthorn Road
Broomall, PA 18900
610-453-1993
Denise.Deska@denisedeska.com

April 10, 2008

Ms. Veronica Jones, MSN, RN
Vice President of Nursing
Susquehanna Health System
1100 Grampian Boulevard
Philadelphia, PA 14706

Dear Ms. Jones:

I saw your ad in *Pennsylvania Nurse,* and I would like to apply for the position of Clinical Practice Coordinator of the Oncology unit. I have just completed my MSN at the University of Pennsylvania with a clinical specialty in oncology. My BSN is from Lycoming College, and I have eight years experience in medical-surgical nursing with the last four in oncology.

I have included a resume and a list of references with contact information. I would welcome the opportunity for an interview.

Thank you for your consideration.

Sincerely yours,

Denise K. Deska

Denise K. Deska, MSN, RN

Enclosures

8.3 Commonly Misspelled Words in a Business Letter

Acceptance	Definitely	Opportunities
Achievement	Equipped	Perceive
Anticipation	Exceptionally	Perseverance
Approximately	Fortunately	Philosophy
Candidate	Immediately	Possess
Commitment	Inconvenience	Practically
Confidential	Irrelevant	Receipt
Conscious	Necessarily	Recommend
Correspondence	Occasionally	Schedule

How can you avoid errors with words with different meanings that look alike or sound alike?

* Use your spell and grammar check.

* Have someone else proof your letter.

See the following box for common errors.

Common Writing Traps

Affect and **effect**

Affect is usually a verb meaning to influence.

Effect as a noun means result; as a verb it means to bring to pass.

The new legislation affected mandatory overtime, and this effect helped nurse recruitment.

Among and between

Among introduces more than two items.

Between introduces two items.

It should be shared among the entire staff.

This matter should be kept between the two of us.

Bring and take

Bring indicates motion toward a person.

Take indicates motion away.

Please bring this water to Mrs. Miller.

Take the dinner tray from the room.

Can and may

Can implies ability

May implies permission.

Jerry may obtain the blood sugar if he can.

Complement and compliment

Complement refers to something that completes.

Compliment refers to praise.

The color of that scarf complements your suit.

He gave me a very nice compliment about my scarf.

Emigrate and immigrate

People *emigrate* or move out of one country.

They *immigrate* or move into another country.

The Irish emigrant was given permission to immigrate to the United States.

Farther and **further**

Farther refers to a physical distance.

Further means more or additional and is used as a time or quantity word

Move that desk farther to the right.

Let's take the point one step further to the next logical conclusion.

Fewer and **less**

Fewer refers to items that you can count.

Less refers to degree or quantity.

There are fewer nurses in the same day surgery unit, and they have less experience than the nurses in the post-anesthesia care unit.

Irregardless and **regardless**

Irregardless is not a standard word and should not be used.

Regardless means despite or in spite of something.

The budget has been predetermined, regardless of what transpires in the meeting.

Me

Me is the object of a verb or preposition.

This problem is between you and me.

They called you and me.

Stationary and **stationery**

Stationary means fixed in place.

Stationery refers to writing materials.

Once correctly installed, the new digital mammography machine remained stationary.

I will write my thank-you notes with my new stationery.

Was and were

Was is used for things in the past.

Were expresses a wish or states a doubtful situation.

I was surprised to find you there.

If I were a college student, I would choose nursing as a career.

Who and whom

Who is used for the person who is the subject of a sentence.

Whom (the objective case of who) refers to the person who has been the object of an action.

Who brought the new equipment?

The new equipment is to be used for whom?

Is a shorter letter more professional than a longer letter?

Yes. Be clear and concise. Don't waste the reader's time with unnecessary information. Read what you have written and eliminate any extra words or data. See *Elements of Style*, the classic grammar book written by William Strunk and E.B. White (2000). This little book is often described as the best primer on writing. It provides more information in less space than almost any other book.

"Do not be tempted by a twenty-dollar word when there is a ten-center handy, ready, and able."

—William Strunk and E.B White

How should you handle the address and salutation of a letter if you do not know the sex of the recipient?

Drop the courtesy title in the address and salutation to avoid risking an unintended insult. For example, use "Pat Stanley" and "Dear Pat Stanley."

TIP

Edit, edit, edit. Eliminate grammar problems, spelling errors, and poor style.

What should you write when you are addressing a position rather than a specific person?

Address the position, such as, "Dear Infection Control Nurse." This is preferred over "To whom it may concern."

Are there any particular phrases that should be avoided when writing?

Yes. See the table below for some windbag phrases and their substitutions.

8.4 Windbag Phrases

WINDBAG PHRASES	CONCISE REPLACEMENTS
Due to the fact that	Because
The reason why is that	Because
As per your request, enclosed please find	I have enclosed
Enclosed herewith	Here is
Until such time	When
As to when	When

Windbag Phrases (continued)

WINDBAG PHRASES	CONCISE REPLACEMENTS
In connection with	About
Subsequent to	After
As to how	How
Any and all	All
Prior to	Before

"Brevity is the soul of wit."

—Shakespeare (from *Hamlet*)

Frequently Asked Questions

 Is it OK to send a thank-you by e-mail?

Only if you plan to follow it with a handwritten note. E-mail is better than no mail, but it is always a second choice to a handwritten note. An e-mail does not send the message that you went out of your way to send your thanks. It appears to be a hasty attempt to cross a task off your to-do list. However, it is OK to use e-mail to thank a colleague for a small favor. This is different from receiving a gift, being taken out for dinner, or following up on an interview.

 When is it unnecessary to RSVP?

If an invitation does not include an RSVP, you do not need to reply. However, it is as rude to ignore an RSVP as it is to not say "please" and "thank you." Some hostesses may indicate "regrets only" as a way of keeping a head count. In this case, unless you indicate otherwise, your attendance is expected.

 Should I type a thank-you note if I have poor handwriting?

No. Print a short note neatly and sign your name. However, if your note is longer than a few sentences, type it.

 Is there a proper way to fold a business letter before inserting it into an envelope?

Yes. A business letter is folded in thirds. Fold the bottom third up first and then fold the top third down. Insert the letter into the envelope so it is right side up and readable when removed from the back of the envelope.

 What do you think of printed holiday cards with no handwritten message?

If you are not going to personalize them, don't waste your time and money sending them. You are not creating a positive impression.

 How do you address an invitation to two people with different surnames who live at the same address?

Each person gets a line for his or her name. If it is a man and a woman, the woman's name is listed first.

 How do you address a letter or thank-you note to a couple where one or both are doctors?

Here are some options:

- ✳ Dr. and Mrs. Brian Myers
- ✳ Dr. Linda Myers and Mr. Brian Myers
- ✳ Dr. Linda Myers and Dr. Brian Myers

** Should I use a comma or a colon after the salutation line in a business letter?**

The colon is preferred practice for most business letters (for example, Dear Ms. Dewar:).

TAKE-AWAY TIPS

✓ Think of a thank-you note as the 5-minute difference between feeling grateful and showing gratitude.

✓ Whenever someone gives you time, advice, a gift, or a helping hand, send a thank-you note.

✓ Brief and to the point is far better than long and wordy.

✓ Neatness counts. Your letter is a stand-in for you.

✓ Err on the side of politeness and use "Ms.," "Mrs.," or "Mr." until you have established a mutual rapport.

✓ Who doesn't enjoy receiving a note in the mail?

✓ Invest in good quality stationery.

✓ Don't use a postage meter when sending thank-you notes. Use a stamp.

✓ A late thank-you note is better than not sending a note at all.

✓ Bad grammar leaves a bad impression.

✓ Proper grammar and spelling demonstrate your attention to detail.

9

*

Jet Setting to Success

Business Travel and Etiquette

Do you:

Know if you should bring along your laptop computer?

Know the best way to get from the airport to your hotel?

Wonder if you should check or carry your luggage on the plane?

Feel uncomfortable eating alone?

Feel concern for your safety?

Know how much to tip when travelling?

There is no doubt that business travel has the potential to be stressful. Things do go wrong, and the unexpected does happen. However, if you know some basics, you will decrease your stress and increase your chance of having an enjoyable trip. Read on to find out how to be a good traveler and how to take your business etiquette along on your trip.

Traveling With Manners

"No act of kindness, no matter how small, is ever wasted."

—Aesop

What does it take to be a good traveler?

A good traveler focuses on three basic objectives:

1. Be prepared.
2. Be self-reliant.
3. Be flexible.

The information in this chapter will help you attain these goals.

If you need to fly out of town for business, who is responsible for scheduling your airline reservations?

This will vary. Some companies will give you guidelines for making your reservations and expect you to do it. The guidelines may include a maximum ticket price and what airport to fly into. Other companies will have a travel department that you must connect with to make your reservations. There is usually an expectation that all tickets are booked at least a month before the event to get the best airfare possible.

Is it a good idea to stick with one air carrier?

If possible and financially prudent, yes. You often get better seats if you are a frequent flyer. In addition, frequent flyers often can board before other passengers, get seats near the front of the plane and, when available, may be offered first-class seats when upgrades are available. And, frequent flyers build up points and can earn free flights.

When your travel plans are finalized, who should get a copy of your itinerary?

The person you are meeting, your office, and your family should get copies. Make sure the itinerary includes the following essential details:

* Flight schedule with name of the airline, flight numbers, and departure and arrival times.

* Name, address, and phone number of your hotel.

* Location and times of your meetings.

* Name and contact information of the person you are meeting.

What can you do to prevent frustration with airplane delays and cancellations?

Be prepared by not expecting everything to go well. Give yourself plenty of time to get to your destination. Never take the last plane out of the airport. If it gets cancelled, you are really stuck. It is best to arrive much earlier than necessary, to allow plenty of time to work or relax before business. Plan to arrive the day before any important event.

What should you do when your flight is cancelled?

This is an unfortunate situation, but handling it effectively is part of the flexibility needed to be a good traveler. Here are some suggestions.

* Do not get angry with the airline service personnel.

* While standing in line to speak to an agent, use your cell phone to call the airline or your travel agent to book another flight.

* Ask the airline if it has any partner airlines to accommodate your travel.

* Inquire about meal tickets and hotel vouchers.

What suggestions do you have to make your flight check-in go smoothly?

This is a stressful event for most travelers. Here are some suggestions:

* Check the status of your flight by phone or on the Web site several hours before leaving your home for the airport. Print out your boarding pass within 24 hours of your departure time.

* Be sure you have photo identification. Use your driver's license or passport.

* Make sure your checked luggage does not exceed the weight restrictions.

* Make sure your carry-on luggage does not exceed the size limitations.

* Check with the transit authority on the policy for packing liquids. Many liquid containers with more than a few ounces are not allowed in carry-on luggage. Your liquids, including toothpaste and creams, must fit into a 1-quart plastic bag.

* Arrive at the airport early. Check the airline's Web site or Transportation Security Administration Web site, http://www.tsa.gov, for suggested check-in times. Many airports advise arriving 1-2 hours before flight time to get through security clearance.

 * For international flights, bring your passport and be at the airport at least 2 hours before flight time. Make sure you are in the right terminal. International departures from large airports such as Chicago O'Hare or New York will often be in a separate terminal, because of the larger aircraft.

* Always check the visa and entry requirements of each country before you book travel or depart. Some countries have regulations regarding travel within a specified time period of the expiration date of the passport. For instance, Singapore will not allow entry to those whose passport expires within 6 months of the date of requested entry.

* Do not have any wrapped gifts in your carry-on luggage.

* Eat before you leave home or bring some food. Few airlines provide food or snacks on regular flights. In some cases, you can purchase a small meal or snack.

* Do not leave your bags unattended or ask anyone to watch your bags.

Is it better to carry on or check your luggage on the plane?

Both have advantages. If your trip is purely business, minimize your packing and carry on your luggage. If your trip is for pleasure, you can pack more things if you check your bag. However, make sure you carry any medications or valuables with you.

Plan for the possibility that your checked luggage may get lost or be delayed. Put some essentials, such as a toothbrush, toothpaste, and possibly a change of underwear, in your carry-on bag or purse.

How should you dress on the plane?

This will depend on when you will meet people at your destination and if you plan to check your bags. If you plan to meet people before you will have the opportunity to change, dress for that meeting. If you are checking your bags, wear something presentable in case your bags get lost. If you are carrying your bags and not meeting anyone until after you have checked in, you have more options for dressing in a casual manner.

Always carry a sweater or jacket. You will be more comfortable in the airport and on the plane.

How much do you tip the skycap at the airport?

Tip $1 per bag for checking your bags. If the skycap carries your bag into the terminal, tip $2 per bag (Fox, 2001). Some airports now charge a fee of $2 per bag, not including tip.

How can you demonstrate professional etiquette while flying?

Because flying can be stressful and you are in close quarters with many others, it is essential to demonstrate good manners. See Table 9.1 for some helpful tips.

 Etiquette Tips for Flyers

✳ Wait your turn when boarding and disembarking the plane.

✳ If your luggage does not fit into the overhead compartment or under the seat in front of you, tell the flight attendant so it can be checked.

✳ Ask your seatmate's permission before adjusting the window shades.

✳ Turn off your cell phone.

✳ Don't block the aisle for more than a few seconds when putting your luggage in the overhead compartment.

✳ Don't crush anyone's belongings in the overhead compartment to squeeze in your belongings.

✳ Don't ask to put your luggage in someone else's foot space.

Etiquette Tips for Flyers

✳ Keep your things in your own space.

✳ Don't stretch out into the aisle.

✳ Nod and say "hello" to your seatmates.

✳ Don't keep talking if the person next to you wants to sleep, work, or read.

✳ Don't try to read the computer screen of people nearby.

✳ Be considerate of the flight attendants (Brody, 2005).

✳ Be considerate of the person seated behind you. In some planes, if you crank your seat back, you can end up in the lap of the person behind you. This is annoying and prevents that person from working on his or her computer.

"Rudeness is the weak man's imitation of strength."

—Lawrence Sterne

What are the options for transportation from the airport to the hotel?

Taxis are a convenient way to get to your hotel, especially if you are in a hurry and it is dark. Before traveling, call the hotel and ask for the usual fare from the airport to the hotel. It is also a good idea to use the Internet to get directions. You will find out the most direct route and the estimated time for travel. Carry small bills in case the driver cannot make change. Tip the driver 15-20% of the fare.

You can also hire a car service. In this case, there will be a car waiting for you and a person standing near the baggage claim area with your name or company name on a sign. Because the cost is determined up front, there are no surprises. You can also pay with your credit card with most car services.

Other options for travel include trains, subways, and buses. Some hotels provide free shuttle services. Find out about available services by calling the hotel ahead of time. If you are attending a conference, this information is usually available in the brochure or with the registration confirmation materials.

How can you demonstrate professional etiquette on trains?

Like airplanes, you are in close quarters with other travelers. Here are some tips:

* Minimize use of your cell phone. Speak softly and briefly if you have to use it. Be aware that cell phones are now prohibited in some train cars.

* Don't distract others who are trying to read or relax.

* Don't spread out your things and tie up seats.

* Offer your seat to disabled or elderly people.

* Be courteous to the conductor.

What travel tips do you recommend for a road trip in your car?

You need to know exactly where you are going, how to get there, and how much time it takes. As with flying, don't make this a last-minute stressor. See Table 9.2 for road-trip tips.

Guide for Road Trips

* Get the exact location of the event, including the zip code.

* Make use of a mapping service, such as MapQuest or Google Maps, for directions.

* Print out your directions in large type for easy reading.

* Rent or purchase a global positioning system (GPS) car navigator.

* Make sure your car is trip-ready. Fix any indicator alerts, such as a low oil level.

* Bring your sunglasses.

* Be aware of your gas level and keep the level above a quarter of a tank.

* Travel with your cell phone.

* Always lock your car doors.

* Park only in well-lit areas.

* If you feel uncomfortable, ask a security guard to walk you to your car.

* Leave only your ignition key with a parking attendant.

Do you have any recommendations for renting a car?

Renting a car should be part of your pre-trip planning. You could get to your destination and not be able to rent a car. Here are some tips:

* Have a copy of your rental car reservation in your hand when you meet the agent.

* Be careful of the agent's push to sell unneeded services. Your own car insurance is usually enough, but be sure to check with your insurance agent if this is your first time to rent a car.

* Do not agree to pay a cheaper gas price for the car rental agency to fill the tank when you return the car, unless you plan to return the car on empty. The rental agency will charge to fill the entire tank, even if you only needed a few gallons. Your best option is usually to fill the car yourself right before you return it to the rental agency and only pay for the gas you used.

* Do not discuss any private business on a cell phone or with a co-worker on the rental car shuttle bus. You never know who is on the bus and how he or she might use your information.

* Check to make sure the gas tank is full before you leave the lot.

* Make sure you have directions before you leave the lot. You can get a map from the rental company. However, it is usually better to bring your own directions from a mapping service such as MapQuest or Google Maps.

* Rent a GPS system to prevent getting lost in an unfamiliar area.

* Try to pick up and return rental vehicles during daylight hours.

* Keep the car doors locked at all times.

* Put your luggage in the trunk.

How do you handle your expenses and reimbursements on a business trip?

Before you begin your trip, find out what will be reimbursed and what the caps are for reimbursement. For example, you may be limited to a per diem of $30, or a meal total of $30. You also may be reimbursed for a shuttle service, but not for a taxi.

Keep receipts for everything. It is helpful to have a designated place for keeping receipts. You will need an itemized hotel bill if you charged your meals to your room. As soon as you return from your trip, make a copy of your receipts and submit your reimbursement form. Some companies have a time limit for submitting these forms.

Take your manners with you on your trip.

Packing With Precision

What suggestions do you have for packing?

Carefully plan your packing. Pack only what you need and leave the rest at home. Mix and match outfits as much as possible. Think of the events and plan your outfits for each one. I find it helpful to place my outfits with accessories out on my bed before placing them in a suitcase. My best idea has been to design and use a travel checklist every time I pack. I cross off anything that does not apply to the trip and then check off everything else as I pack it. See Tables 9.3 and 9.4 for suggestions on developing your own customized list.

Have a cosmetic kit or shaving kit always packed and ready to go. Refill necessary items after each trip.

Packing List for Personal Items

Program/Event

Suit

Shirt/extra shirt

Shoes

Stockings or socks

Underwear

Jewelry

Night Clothes

Pajamas/nightgown

Robe

Slippers

Fitness

Swim cap, swimsuit, and goggles

Gym shirt

Sneakers/running shoes

Jacket for outside exercise

Sunscreen

Gym pants or shorts

Personal Items

Make-up kit

Toiletries

Shaving kit

Curling iron

Contact lenses

Miscellaneous

Cell phone

Cell phone charger

Hat

Sunglasses, reading glasses

Earplugs

Reading materials

José was flying during a thunderstorm. When he got to his final destination, he was relieved to retrieve his luggage. However, when he unpacked in his hotel, all of his clothes were wet. Everything had to be cleaned. Because of this experience, he now packs his clothing inside a plastic drycleaner's bag. It doesn't take up any room, and it keeps his clothes dry.

9.4   **Packing List for Business Items**

Hardware Essentials

Computer

Computer power source

Program loaded on computer

Program backed up on flash drive

Extension cord

Travel Documents

Hotel reservations

Travel directions

Airline reservations

Photo identification

Passport

Contact information

Presentation

Presentation notes

Printed copies of your presentation (PowerPoint®)

Copy of the handouts

Program details

Miscellaneous

Business cards

Tablet

Highlighter

Calendar

Writing utensils

Do you have any recommendations for organizing my suitcase?

Fold all of your items and place them in reusable, sealable bags such as Ziploc® bags. Nothing will get wet and nothing will spill (T.N. Pagana, 2008). This is a great way to organize and group items. For example, put all underwear in one bag.

Fold and then roll each garment separately, and then tuck into a quart, gallon, or 2-gallon sealable plastic bag. This cuts down on wrinkling and allows you to quickly find your items.

When rolling pants, start at the hem and roll up. When folding
shirts and sweaters, fold a section on each side with the sleeves back,
and then roll from the bottom up.

Should I bring an iron?

No. Most hotels have an iron and ironing board in the closet. If not,
they can usually supply them. You can call ahead and verify this.
If you unpack your clothes and find they are wrinkled, try hanging
them in a hot shower. The steam will usually remove the wrinkles.

 If you are traveling overseas, you probably won't have access to an
iron. Also, you will need to bring an adapter for electrical items because of different electrical currents. As an example, you will not be
able to use a blow dryer without an adapter.

Marianne was traveling for business and stayed in a very nice hotel.
She was getting ready 40 minutes before she needed to leave her
room. Having just showered, she tried to dry her hair with the blow
dryer, but it did not work. By the time she received a replacement,
she had only 10 minutes to dry and style her hair. She had to rush
out of her room to be on time for her meeting. Now, she tries the
blow dryer as soon as she checks in.

Hotels

What are some safety tips when staying alone in hotels?

This is an important issue, especially for women traveling alone. See
the box on the next page for safety tips when staying in a hotel.

Hotel Safety Tips

- Keep your room number private. If the bellman asks for your room number, show your key rather than say the number.

- If the desk clerk makes your room number public, ask for a different room.

- When shopping in the gift shop or eating in the dining room, don't mention your room number when you are charging something to your room.

- Have the bellman enter your room with you and stay while you check the room. This is especially important if it is dark and you are fearful.

- If you are uncomfortable about the location of your room, ask to have it changed. It's a good idea to ask for a room that is not on the ground floor when you make your reservation or when you are checking in.

- Do not open the door if anyone knocks. Call the front desk to verify any room work or service.

- Bolt the door and apply the safety latch.

- If there is a sliding door, make sure it has a safety latch and a metal bar.

- If your room has a connecting door, make sure it is locked. If possible, try to book a room without a connecting door.

- Don't leave the door open with the latch lock if you leave the room to get ice.

- Always have your room key out and ready to use as you walk to your room.

- Use the room safe to secure your valuables.

- Make sure your door closes and locks every time you leave the room.

- Keep a light on in the room when you leave, so it is not dark when you return.

- If the hotel fitness center does not have an attendant, use the facility only when other people are around.

- Use valet parking if you arrive late and have to walk through a dark parking lot (Rickenbacher, 2004).

- If you are leaving your room after it's been cleaned, put out the "do not disturb" sign so it appears that someone is in the room.

✓ *Good Idea!*

Margaret was traveling to speak at a conference. She arrived at her hotel early and checked in. When she got to her room, she found it was not part of the main hotel. It also did not have an inside entrance, and the room was on the ground floor. Not feeling safe, she returned to the registration desk to discuss her concerns. She was switched to a nicer room with a safer inside entry. Safety is a number one concern for women traveling alone, and hotels will do their best to accommodate solo travelers.

TIP

Always be alert and aware of your surroundings.

If you need to hold a business meeting at the hotel, is it OK to use your hotel room?

No. Arrange to use a meeting room. Or, meet in a dining room. It is too personal to meet in your hotel room, especially with a member of the opposite sex.

Should you bring an alarm clock?

This depends. Most hotels have alarm clocks. Check the clock when you get into the room. The alarm may still be set by a previous occupant. If you cannot figure out how to set the alarm, call the front desk. For some people, it is more convenient to bring a small travel alarm that they know is dependable and know how to use.

TIP

If you need more light in your hotel room, call housekeeping and request a lamp.

Do you recommend using the wake-up call service?

Yes. This is a great idea. However, have a back-up strategy. Sometimes, the call system goes down. Also, be certain to hang up the phone properly or it will not ring in the morning. Use the alarm in your room or on your cell phone as a back-up.

Do you need to bring your computer to a hotel?

This varies. Bring your computer if you need it for your work. Otherwise, many hotels have a business center with computers. In some cases, there is a small fee for usage. Call in advance to learn about computer and printer usage at your hotel.

Is Internet service available in most hotels?

Yes, but it is not free in most hotels. Often the charge is $10-$15 per day. This is billed on a 24-hour period or billed as a full day until the next day's checkout time. Interestingly, low-cost hotels often have free Internet service.

✗ *Faux Pas*

Kathy and her 78-year-old father were checking out of a hotel when Kathy saw her dad putting all of the snack items in his suitcase. He thought the snack items were free and did not realize that every snack or mini-bar item missing from the room is charged to the room bill. The room items are also priced much higher than those in the gift shop.

How can you expedite checking out of a hotel?

You should receive a copy of your bill under your door on the morning of checkout. Review all of the charges and read the checkout instructions. In many cases, you can call a number and indicate the time when you are vacating the room. You may also be able to check out using the TV or a kiosk in the hotel lobby. If there are any items on your bill that you are unsure of, call or go to the front desk to discuss them. Everything will be charged to the credit card you have on file, and your balance should be $0 on your statement.

If you are sharing a hotel room, how can you get a receipt for your expenses?

This can easily be done at the front desk. The clerk can separate the charges and give both of you an individualized, itemized receipt.

Are there etiquette guidelines for tipping in a hotel?

Yes. It is a good idea to travel with a lot of $1 bills for tipping. Here are some suggestions for tipping:

* Maid who cleans your room: $2 per night.

* Doorman who carries your bag: $1 per bag.

* Bellman who carries your bags to your room: $1 to $2 per bag.

* Concierge who gives you a map and directions: no tip.

* Concierge who makes dinner reservations for you: $10-$20.

* Concierge who finds hard-to-get theatre tickets for you: $10-$20 per ticket.

* Doorman who hails a cab: $1.

* Wait staff in a restaurant: 15-20% of the tab (excluding tax).

* Room service wait staff: no tip or $1. The gratuity is usually added to the bill whenever you order room service.

* Valet parking: $1-$2 (Fox, 2001; Post & Post, 1999).

Frequently Asked Questions

 Should I carry my blow dryer on a trip?

No. Most hotels have these in the room. Call the hotel to verify this.

 If you are traveling with a person of honor, who gets into the cab first?

You should get in first so you are the last out and can pay the driver. The person of honor should have the rear seat closest to the curb. This avoids the person needing to slide across the seat.

(?) How much should I tip a cab driver?

The usual tip is 15-20% of the fare on the meter. Add $1 per bag if the driver loads your bags in and out of the trunk.

(?) Is it OK to bring your spouse on a business trip?

Yes, if he or she knows that business comes first.

(?) If I am traveling alone, should I order room service and eat in my room?

No, unless you want to. It is perfectly acceptable to eat by yourself in the dining room. Bring a magazine or book to read until your food arrives. It is common for travelers to eat alone.

TAKE-AWAY TIPS

✓ While traveling, maintain a confident but low-key profile.

✓ Trust your instincts. If you feel uncomfortable, leave.

✓ Keep your travel clothing simple, lightweight, and wrinkle-free.

✓ Don't forget to pack clothes for evenings.

✓ If you do not know what to wear, ask your host.

✓ Carry a prescription for needed medications.

✓ Carry a lens prescription for glasses or contacts.

✓ Make a copy of your itinerary and give it to a family member or friend.

✓ If possible, avoid changing money at airports, where it is more expensive. The best place to change money is at a local bank.

✓ Have all luggage identified inside and outside.

✓ Take inconveniences in stride.

10

✳

Going Global

Business Etiquette Around the World

Do you:

Wonder how you should dress for business in another country?

Know if you should give a gift to your hostess?

Know that some gestures can be offensive, but don't know which ones to avoid?

Know the handshaking etiquette for women?

Wonder how to present and receive a business card?

Know the dining etiquette differences in other countries?

Just as with business travel, preparation, self-reliance, and flexibility are key components of a successful international travel experience. However, international travel and interactions are complicated by cultural differences in etiquette. Each culture has its own traditions, rules, and priorities. It is important to learn about these variations before setting out on your trip.

Important Note to Nontravelers:

You may think you will not get any benefit out of reading this chapter. Wrong! As a health care professional, you interact with patients and providers from diverse cultural backgrounds. Reading this chapter will enhance your cultural awareness and sensitivity in your interactions with others.

"Manners must adorn knowledge and smooth its way through the world."

—Lord Chesterfield, 1748

Basic Preparations

What is an "ugly American," and how can you avoid being called one during your travels?

The term originated as the title of a 1958 book called *The Ugly American*, by Eugene Burdick and William Lederer. The term describes Americans abroad who are perceived as arrogant, demeaning, and thoughtless. For example, you may come off sounding superior and judgmental with comments such as "I can't believe this restaurant does not have ice cubes" or "These people seem lazy taking a siesta every day after lunch."

Educating yourself before you travel and having an appreciation for cultural differences can help you avoid this stigma. Remember, the American way is not the only way. Your behavior should not be offensive to the people whose country you are visiting.

What are some suggestions for etiquette research as you make your travel plans?

Remember that what is polite and appropriate in one culture may be offensive in another. Refer to the topics in Table 10.1. Research these topics before you leave home. Use the Internet or get a guidebook. See the resources listed near the end of the chapter.

TIP

Ignorance of business etiquette protocol is simply not acceptable in the global arena.

10.1 Research Etiquette Before Travel

✶ Appropriate greetings

✶ Handshake, kissing, or bowing customs

✶ Gift-giving etiquette

✶ Dress codes

✶ Gestures

✶ Eye contact

✶ Religious beliefs and customs

✶ Business interactions

✶ Social structure, such as the role of women in the culture

✶ Relationship between bosses and subordinates

✶ Concept of time (being prompt or late)

What are some basic facts you should learn about a country before your trip?

Table 10.2 covers most of the basics to investigate, so you can feel more comfortable and appreciate your travel adventures. If you do your homework, you will avoid the lack of preparation that is a shortcoming for many U.S. travelers.

 Country Facts to Research and Know Before You Go

* The correct name of the country (for example, the Czech Republic)

* The nation's capital

* The form of government

* The names of the top government officials

* Types of religion

* National holidays that may fall during your trip

* Dietary laws

* Leading industries

* Type of currency and exchange rates

* Prominent geographical features (for example, the Great Wall of China)

* Famous cultural landmarks (for example, the Catacombs)

* Famous men and women (for example, writers, musicians, artists)

* Popular sports (Post & Post, 1999)

Currency Conversions

Go online to a Web site that calculates currency conversions. For example, go to www.oanda.com and click on the "FXConverter."

- Enter your countries and click "convert now."
- Then click on "Traveler's Cheatsheet." Print out this conversion table and tape it to one side of a small index card.
- Then, click on the "Reverse FXCheatSheet." Print and tape this table to the other side of the index card.
- This information is invaluable. You can estimate currency conversions without needing a calculator (T.N. Pagana, 2008).

Should you try to speak the language in a foreign country?

Yes, demonstrate your respect by learning a few words. Even if you mispronounce the words, people will appreciate your effort. Here are some words to try to learn:

- ✳ Hello
- ✳ Goodbye
- ✳ Please
- ✳ Thank you
- ✳ Good morning
- ✳ Good afternoon
- ✳ Good night
- ✳ Excuse me

Carry a pocket dictionary to help you communicate with people who do not speak English.

Do you have any suggestions for working with translators?

Yes, if you are using a translator to communicate with someone, look at and speak directly to the person instead of the interpreter. Avoid jokes, because humor does not translate well. You could easily offend someone.

How do you know how to dress for a business meeting?

This is definitely an area to investigate before packing. In general, dress on the conservative side until you see what your international colleagues are wearing. In most circumstances, women should avoid skirts or dresses above the knee. Women should be especially conservative in deeply religious countries. You should carefully investigate appropriate dress in these countries. A good place to begin your investigation is with the country link on the United States Department of State Web site (www.state.gov).

If you make an etiquette blunder, what should you do?

Your mistake may be obvious from someone's comments, expression, or body language. Apologize immediately. If you do not know what you did, say: "Please help me. Let me know what I did, so I won't do it again." Demonstrate a humble and respectful attitude. It is not acceptable to simply say, "I didn't know."

If you are hosting a visitor from another country, how can you be a gracious host?

You can be a gracious host if you take time to learn about the person's culture. Here are some guidelines to ensure a nice visit:

* Know the visitor's usual method of greeting.

* Learn about the visitor's customs and values.

* Meet or send someone to meet the person at the airport.

* Ask about dietary restrictions in advance, if possible.

* Send flowers or a basket of food to the person's room. Be culturally sensitive when making your selection.

* Arrange for transportation during the person's visit.

* Plan interesting things for the person to do.

* Invite the person to your home for dinner (Pachter, 2006b).

Introductions

How do you know how to greet an international business associate?

If you are not sure how to greet the person, start with a handshake or follow his or her lead. If the person greets you with a kiss, follow suit. You may offend the person if you pull away. A bow or a hug may be appropriate in other cultures.

How does handshake etiquette differ around the world?

In the United States, a firm handshake is used to communicate confidence and self-assurance. Don't judge people from other cultures by their handshakes. Here are some things to learn:

* Who initiates the handshake? (It may be the most senior person.)

* Do men wait for women to extend their hand? (Yes, in many European countries.)

* Can men shake a woman's hand? (Not if they are Muslim or Hindu.)

* Should the grip be gentle or firm? (In Denmark, Finland, Ireland, Norway, and Sweden, the handshakes are firm but brief. In China, the handshakes are softer and longer.)

* Is a bow the equivalent of a handshake? (Yes, in Japan and some other Asian countries.)

If a bow is used instead of a handshake, who bows first?

In a rank-conscious society such as Japan, the person of lower rank bows first and lowest.

What should I do if someone ignores my handshake?

Gently drop your hand back to your side. There are many cultural preferences and sensitivities that impact the handshake. For example, in the Hindu culture, contact between men and women is avoided, and men do not shake hands with a woman. There also may be physical limitations or sickness issues.

Is business card etiquette different around the world?

Yes. If you'll be traveling in a foreign country for business, do some research on business card etiquette before leaving home.

People in some countries (such as Germany) are impressed by education and like to see all degrees and titles above the bachelor's degree. In Saudi Arabia, the card should be printed in English on one side and Arabic on the other. When traveling to Poland, bring plenty of cards and give one to everyone you meet (K.D. Pagana, 2006d).

Business cards should be presented with the content face up and readable. There are many variations associated with business card etiquette when traveling internationally. For example, in China, hold the card with both hands when offering it. In India, the right hand presents and receives the card. In Japan, business cards are given with one hand, but received with both hands (K.D. Pagana, 2007a).

Conversations and Networking

What topics of conversation should you avoid in your travels?

Avoid discussing religion and politics. It is easy to offend people with what may seem like a harmless remark. If someone tries to engage you in a conversation about politics or religion, say something like, "I've learned never to discuss politics or religion." Then, change the subject. For example, ask about a cultural landmark.

Are there any American expressions, jargon, or idioms to avoid?

Yes. Even if the person understands and speaks English, he or she may be confused by certain expressions. If you say something and get a confused look, think of another way of saying it. Listed below are some examples of phrases that do not translate well.

* ASAP
* Twenty-four-seven (24/7)
* Shoot yourself in the foot
* Take your foot out of your mouth
* It's a double-header
* Think outside the box
* Hit the ground running
* Dead as a doornail

Should you be concerned about using gestures?

Yes. There are several gestures that can be misunderstood or considered insulting. Here are some examples to avoid:

* The "okay" sign (making a circle with thumb and forefinger and having three raised fingers) is offensive in many countries, such as Brazil. It means "money" in Japan and means "worthless" in France (Pachter, 2006b).

* Thumbs up. (Considered rude in Egypt.)

* "V" for victory sign, especially with the palm facing inward. (This is offensive in Great Britain.)

* Pointing or snapping your fingers.

* Waving your hand with your arm raised (may be misunderstood as "no").

Is it considered friendly to use first names when traveling?

No. This informality is common in the United States, but it will probably be considered disrespectful when traveling abroad. Instant familiarity usually does not make a good impression in other parts of the world. Never begin using first names until given permission. In fact, you may not ever be given permission. Address people by their proper titles. Titles such as doctor and professor are highly valued in Germany, Italy, and many other countries (Whitmore, 2005).

TIP In general, business people should follow the customs of the country they are in.

How do you know how much eye contact is appropriate?

Investigate this. In the United States, people are encouraged to look into the eyes of the person they are communicating with. In many Asian countries, however, looking away is a sign of respect. In France, you may be looked at more intently than you expect (Pachter, 2006b).

How can you develop effective relationships in a business setting?

Focus on relationships. Don't try to push past relationship building to get to business. The "getting to know you" phase builds trust. Executives in regions such as Asia, Latin America, and the Middle East place a premium on relationship protocol. In Japan, for example, you may be invited for tea several times before someone decides whether or not to do business with you (Whitmore, 2005).

The American business practice of "getting right down to business" is not shared by other cultures. Do not expect other cultures to do business the "American way."

How do you handle personal space issues when traveling?

Handle this with care. Be aware that proximity when conversing with someone is dictated by custom. The average "personal space" distance in the United States is approximately 3 feet. In Italy and Argentina, it's closer. In Japan, it's farther away (Pachter, 2006b).

What key etiquette ideas can you learn by observation?

You can learn how people treat each other, act, and dress by being alert and watching those around you. For example, in some cultures, you should not put your hands on your lap during a meal. Notice if people rest their wrists on the edge of the table.

Notice how a diner signals for the wait staff. If you do not understand why something is done, it is OK to ask. If you do not know what utensil you should use at a meal, follow the example of the native host or guest.

Should you accept social invitations when on business in another country?

Yes. If you are invited somewhere, go and enjoy the experience. You will get a better understanding of the culture. If the invitation is to a home, be sure to bring a gift for the hostess. If you refuse an invitation, your host may feel insulted. That can have a negative impact on your business relationship.

✔ *Good Idea!*

Monika traveled with her family to the Ukraine and met many relatives. She was surprised at dinner when a large bowl of soup was placed in the center of the table and everyone was given a spoon. Although she wanted to ask for her own bowl, she followed the example of her hosts. That is the kind of flexibility and tolerance needed for traveling abroad.

Dining and Drinking Etiquette

What are some differences in dining etiquette?

This is a key area for research. Many business discussions take place over a meal. You don't want to be caught off guard with your actions or your expressions. Here are some examples:

* You may have to sit on the floor and eat with your hands. You may be served food that looks slimy or has eyes. You may offend your host if you do not eat the food.

* Observe how people ask for more food and how they signal when they have had enough. For example, in Thailand, leaving food on your plate means you are finished and the food was delicious. In the Cambodian culture, cleaning your plate means you still want more food. In Japan, cleaning your plate means you appreciate the food (Whitmore, 2005).

* Don't comment on table manners. Be aware of your nonverbal expressions. Good table manners vary from country to country. For example, making a slurping noise while eating is acceptable to the Japanese (Pachter, 2006b).

* Mealtimes vary. If you are the visitor, you must adapt. For example, in Spain, the dinner hour is usually much later than 7 p.m.

* It is proper etiquette to remain standing until shown where to sit. For example, in Japan, an honored guest sits at the center of the table furthest from the door and begins eating first.

TIP

Carry a hand sanitizer with you. Not all bathrooms have soap.

* In some countries, such as Germany, you may see people cutting food with a fork. This compliments the chef by showing the food is tender.

You can learn a lot by observing and following the actions of the hosts.

Faux Pas

When Dennis was traveling in the Middle East, he was a guest at a large banquet. Each time he finished eating his food—when he "cleaned his plate"—he was served another helping. Because the server wanted to be polite, he kept adding food to Dennis's plate. Dennis finally learned that when you are finished eating, you should leave food on your plate.

Faux Pas

Roberto invited a colleague and his spouse from the hospital to his home for dinner. The couple was from Turkey. Roberto's wife made her dinner specialty—flank steak rolled up with pieces of bacon. Unfortunately, the guests could not eat the meat because of the bacon.

What should you do if you are the guest of honor in a foreign country and are served an unknown local delicacy?

Try the food. If you leave it on your plate without trying it, you may insult your host. In some cases, your host may wait for you to take a bite before he or she begins. Keep in mind that acceptance of food and drinks implies acceptance of the host in many countries.

Only ask about a particular food or what is in a particular meal if you have allergies or need to be on a special diet. Be prepared to communicate this information in a clear and respectful manner. If possible, try to communicate dietary restrictions in advance of the meal.

If you are hosting a dinner for international visitors, what foods are considered taboo?

Check this out before you plan the meal. You can ask the person if there are any foods that he or she does not eat. This consideration is very important and demonstrates respect for other cultures. For example, Muslims and Jews do not eat pork. Hindus do not eat beef.

What is considered acceptable for drinking alcohol?

Don't consume too much. Observe and respect the local customs. In some areas, you will be encouraged to drink. For example, drinking wine is an important part of a European meal. If you drink, be smart about it. If you do not drink alcohol, have a soda with a lime or lemon. Note that it is against religious principles to drink alcohol in many Middle Eastern countries. Don't drink if your host does not drink.

✗ Faux Pas

An American college professor was traveling with a group of her students in London. One evening before leaving a pub, she paid the bill and left a tip. A few minutes later, the bartender handed her a piece of paper with a time and his address. He assumed the tip was a proposition! Her students enjoyed telling that story at home.

Gift Giving

How do you know if you need a gift?

Gift-giving customs are tricky and need to be researched. For example, expensive gifts in China may be considered a bribe. In the Middle East, gifts are exchanged with the right hand because the left hand is used for hygiene.

If you are dining at someone's home, you should bring a hostess gift. Some countries require a business gift. Japan, for example, does, but Germany does not.

How can you give the right gift?

Research gift-giving customs ahead of time. It is hard to go wrong with nice pens, chocolates, toys for children, local crafts from your area, or illustrated books from your country.

Sometimes a gift can have a negative meaning. Here are some examples to avoid:

* China: A clock is associated with funerals.

* England: White lilies are only for funerals.

* Germany: Red flowers are only for lovers.

* Saudi Arabia: Alcohol is illegal.

* Mexico: Yellow flowers symbolize death.

How do you know when you should open a gift?

Etiquette also dictates whether or not to open a gift in another country.

* In China, it is inappropriate to open a gift when you receive it. By not opening it, you show that the giving of the gift is more valuable than the actual item (Pachter, 2006b).

* In some cultures, such as South Korea, the gift initially will not be accepted. Be persistent, because the refusal is part of the ritual.

* In Muslim countries, your left hand is considered unclean. Do not give a gift with your left hand.

* In Japan, gift giving is a refined art with many symbolic meanings. It is best to seek guidance from an advisor or a Japanese friend. For example, gifts should be wrapped in lightly tinted paper, not white paper, as it symbolizes death. They should be given and received with both hands. They are opened after the donor has departed.

"A traveler of taste will notice that the wise are polite all over the world, but the fool only at home."

—Oliver Goldsmith

Social Taboos

The examples below will give you an idea of the wide variety of potential faux pas that can occur with international travel. You will see blunders related to communication, body language, gestures, personal space, and dining. Use these general guidelines to develop awareness and to serve as a starting point for your country-specific research. This information will enable you to present yourself to the best of your ability.

Australia

* Don't imitate Australians by saying "G'day, mate" instead of "hello." (It may be taken as patronizing.)

Argentina

* It is rude to yawn in public or eat while walking down the street.

* Placing your hands on your hips is interpreted as a challenge.

* Don't put your feet up on any furniture.

Canada

* The "V" for victory sign is taken as an insult when flashed with the palm inward.

* In some areas, it is bad manners to eat while walking down the street.

* Don't be boastful.

Germany

* Never place a business call to a person's home. (Family and business are kept separate.)

* The "okay" sign is considered obscene.

* Keep your hands out of your pockets.

* Don't wave or call out a person's name in a public place.

* Don't chew gum while talking to someone.

* Punctuality is the norm and is expected.

Great Britain

* Avoid the expression "What do you do?" (Inquiring about a person's livelihood is considered intrusive and rude.)

* Don't talk business at social events.

* Men should wear shoes with laces, not loafers.

Mexico

* Mexicans like to get close. It is rude to pull away when talking.

* Keep your hands out of your pockets.

* Don't stand with your hands on your hips. This suggests aggressiveness.

Saudi Arabia

* The "thumbs up" sign is considered rude.

* Don't discuss religion, politics, or sex.

* Don't pull away if a Saudi colleague embraces you or holds your hand.

* Never show bare shoulders, stomach, calves, or thighs.

* Never show the bottoms of your feet.

* Don't eat with the left hand. (It is considered unclean and used for hygiene.)

Turkey

* Don't cross your legs or show the soles of your shoes.

* Show respect to elders. Shake hands with the oldest person first.

* Stand when an older person enters the room.

* Don't cross your arms when facing someone.

* Keep your hands out of your pockets.

Poland

* Avoid shouting. Poles speak softly.

* Don't put your hands on your lap when dining. Keep your hands above the table.

Japan

* Avoid physical contact after the initial handshake.

* Don't look people directly in the eye. (It invades their privacy.)

* Never boast. (A self-effacing manner is preferred.)

* Never say "no" or "I can't do it." The Japanese prefer not to use the word "no." (This can confuse negotiations.)

Venezuela

* Avoid being too attentive to someone of the opposite sex, because your intentions can be misconstrued (Post & Post, 1999).

* Avoid slouching when seated.

* Don't dominate the conversation. Venezuelans like to be in control.

Where can you get information on topics such as gift-giving customs, social expectations, and cultural taboos?

Here are some valuable resources:

* Morrison, R & Conaway, W.A. (2006). *Kiss, bow, or shake hands: The bestselling guide to doing business in more than 60 countries.* 2nd edition. Avon, MA: Adams Media.

* www.executiveplanet.com

* www.cyborlink.com

Travel Safety

How can you ensure your safety, especially when traveling alone?

Here are some suggestions to follow:

* Don't be taken by surprise. Always be alert.

* Appearing timid or scared makes you look like a victim. Walk with confidence.

* Avoid walking in alleys or deserted areas.

* At night, walk in well-lit areas.

* Choose an ATM in a busy public place.

* Plan your ATM visits during the day (Rickenbacher, 2004).

Is it safe to use local transportation?

It may be safer to travel with the locals. Pickpockets and terrorists may not target local buses as much as tourist buses. Local transportation is a great way to get a feel for the culture of a country. You get to see what the local people wear and talk about (if you can understand them).

Local transportation may not be your best option if you need to get somewhere by a certain time. Frequent stopping results in slower travel (T.N. Pagana, 2008).

How can you prevent being a pickpocket target?

Look confident and goal-oriented, even if you happen to be lost or nervous. Use a money belt to keep your passport and money hidden. Keep your expensive electronic gadgets or jewelry out of sight and away from easy-access pockets. It is a good idea to leave these items at home so you won't worry about their getting lost or stolen (T.N. Pagana, 2008).

TIP

If you feel unsafe, follow your intuition and remove yourself from the situation.

What should you do if you are lost?

Don't panic. Go inside somewhere safe, and then look at your map or ask someone for help. Avoid looking confused while out in a public area. It may make you an easy target for thieves (T.N. Pagana, 2008).

What should you do if you have an emergency?

In case of an emergency, contact the United States embassy or consulate immediately. You should be sure you have the location and contact information for the embassy or consulate before you leave home. If you need the number of an English-speaking doctor, the consulate can give you one. If you get in trouble with the police, the consulate can help you.

Frequently Asked Questions

 Can you use the American style of dining when traveling in Europe?

Yes, but be aware that almost everyone else will be using the Continental style of dining.

 What should you do if you lose your passport in a foreign country?

Report your loss to the nearest United States embassy or consulate, or to the local police. It is easier to replace a passport if you have a photocopy of the data page. If you are traveling with someone, give him or her a copy of your passport. It is also a good idea to have a scanned version of your passport available via Web mail or online in some other way that you can access if you need to.

 How do you know if you need a visa for traveling abroad?

Call the consulate or embassy of the country you want to visit.

If you do not understand why someone does something in a certain way, is it OK to ask him or her?

Yes. Polite questions show you have an interest in another culture. This will help build relationships.

 Is it OK to use humor when conversing with people abroad?

It is better not to use humor, because humor is subjective. Some jokes do not translate well and could cause offense or confusion.

 Is it acceptable to wear "native" clothing when attending a business meeting in another country?

No. This is inappropriate unless encouraged by your hosts.

 Is it appropriate to help yourself to the food at a business meal?

No. Helping yourself is an American custom. Wait until food is offered.

 When traveling out of the country, is gift giving a nice touch?

Gift giving is required in some countries. Find this out before you travel, and also learn what gifts are appropriate.

 I am planning a trip to Japan. Should I learn how to use chopsticks?

Yes. Learn and practice using them before you travel. Don't point with them. Don't pierce food with them. When you are taking a break to drink or talk, rest them on the chopstick rest.

Where should I put my hands when dining?

In the United States, it is OK to place a hand on your lap. However, in many countries (such as France and Poland), the hands are kept above the table. It is inappropriate to put them on your lap.

TAKE-AWAY TIPS

✓ **Think of international travel as an adventure, an opportunity, and a learning experience.**

✓ **The old adage "When in Rome, do as the Romans do" is true.**

✓ **Respect cultural differences.**

✓ **Don't brag about American culture. This is rude.**

✓ **It is not acceptable to make a mistake and simply say, "I didn't know."**

✓ **Refrain from using first names without permission.**

✓ **The American way isn't the only way. Nor, is it always the best way.**

References

Brody, M. (2005). *Professional impressions: Etiquette for everyone, every day* (3rd ed.). Jenkintown, PA: Career Skills Press.

Brown, R.E., & Johnson, D.A. (2004). *The power of handshaking.* Sterling, VA: Capital Books.

Fox, S. (2001). *Business etiquette for dummies.* New York: Wiley Publishing.

Headley, C.M. (2007). Keeping your elbows off your career table. *Nephrology Nursing Journal, 34*(3), 357-358.

Human Factors and Ergonomics Society. (2005, January 28). Hands-on or hands-free, using a cell phone while driving is not safe, researchers find. *HFES News.* Retrieved April 10, 2008, from http://www.hfes.org/web/DetailNews.aspx?ID=72

Kintish, W. (2006). *I hate networking! Discover the secrets of confident and effective networkers.* Manchester, Ontario, Canada: JAM Publications.

Krames, J.A. (2002). *The Rumsfeld way: Leadership wisdom of a battle-hardened maverick.* New York: McGraw-Hill.

Lower, J. (2007). Creating a culture of civility in the workplace: Use these 7 challenges to clean up a toxic work environment. *American Nurse Today, 2*(9), 49-52.

Mitchell, M. (2000). *The complete idiot's guide to etiquette* (2nd ed.). Indianapolis, IN: Alpha Books.

Pachter, B. (2006a). *New rules @ work: 79 etiquette tips, tools, and techniques to get ahead and stay ahead.* New York: Prentice Hall.

Pachter, B. (2006b). *When the little things count: …And they always count.* New York: Marlowe & Company.

Pagana, K.D. (2005a). Dining etiquette: A necessary ingredient for the true professional. *Create the Future Through Renewal,* 2(6).

Pagana, K.D. (2005b). Get in good with the gatekeepers: Tips for avoiding business call blunders. *Pharmaceutical Representative,* 35(9), 44-45.

Pagana, K.D. (2006a). Blunder-free business meals. *American Nurse Today,* 1(3), 61-62.

Pagana, K.D. (2006b). *Bread, butter & beyond: Dining etiquette.* Williamsport, PA: LAYCO Publishing.

Pagana, K.D. (2006c). Business etiquette blunders quiz. *Business Credit,* 108(10), 34-35.

Pagana, K.D. (2006d). Do you need a business card? *American Nurse Today,* 1(2), 47.

Pagana, K.D. (2007a). Business card etiquette: Leaving the right impression. *Networking Times,* 6(3), 28-29.

Pagana, K.D. (2007b). Crossing your 'T's and dotting your 'I's: Professional etiquette in nursing. In C.M. Headley (Ed.), *Career fulfillment in nephrology nursing: Your guide to professional development* (2nd ed.). Pitman, NY: Anthony J. Jannetti.

Pagana, K.D. (2007c). E-mail etiquette: 17 tips for professional communication. *American Nurse Today,* 2(7), 45.

Pagana, K.D. (2007d). The etiquette advantage: The nurse's toolbox. *Journal of Continuing Education in Nursing,* 38(3), 105-106.

Pagana, K.D. (2008). Voice mail etiquette: Make sure your phone messages send the right message. *American Nurse Today,* 3(2), 40.

Pagana, K.D. (in press a). Cell phone etiquette: How to make cell phones a blessing and not a curse. *American Nurse Today.*

Pagana, K.D. (in press b). Tips for handling phone interviews. *American Nurse Today.*

Pagana, T.N. (2008). *Tips for the thrifty traveler: How to travel the world cheaply, easily, & safely.* Williamsport, PA: LAYCO Publishing.

Post, E., & Post, P. (1999). *Emily Post's the etiquette advantage in business.* New York: Harper Collins.

Rickenbacher, C. (2004). *Be on your best behavior.* Dallas, TX: Brown Books.

Sabath, A. (2002). *Business etiquette: 101 ways to conduct business with charm & savvy* (2nd ed.). Franklin Lakes, NJ: Career Press.

Smolenski, M.C. (2002). *Playing the credentials game.* Retrieved November 11, 2007, from http://community.nursingspectrum. com/MagazineArticles/article.cfm?AID=8388

Spade, K. (2004). *Manners: Always gracious, sometimes irreverent.* New York: Simon & Schuster.

Strunk, W., & White, E.B. (2000). *The elements of style* (4th ed.). Needham Heights, MA: Allyn & Bacon.

Whitmore, J. (2005). *Business class: Etiquette essentials for success at work.* New York: St. Martin's Press.

Resources for International Etiquette

Morrison, R., & Conaway, W.A. (2006). *Kiss, bow, or shake hands: The bestselling guide to doing business in more than 60 countries* (2nd ed.). Avon, MA: Adams Media.

www.executiveplanet.com: Provides free information on business dress, topics of conversation, gift giving, entertaining, etc.

www.cyborlink.com: Provides free information on country facts, appearance, behavior, communication, resources, etc.

Business Etiquette Quiz Answers

1. Salad plates and all food to the left of the entrée plate belong to you.

2. True. Remember you are communicating with a person, not a computer.

3. False. A suit with pants or a skirt is professional for women.

4. False. Women shouldn't wear excessive amounts of jewelry.

5. False. E-mail is better than no mail, but it is always a second choice to a handwritten thank-you note. A handwritten note demonstrates good people skills.

6. False. This is rude. Jot the information on a piece of paper.

7. False. "Business" is always the number one item on the menu at a business meal. Your social skills, dinner manners, and level of sophistication are all being evaluated.

8. The VP of nursing is the person of honor and should be mentioned first.

9. False. This is a no-brainer. See Chapter 5 for tips for cell phone usage.

10. True. This avoids getting caught off-guard and having to stammer and stutter.

11. Repeat your name with the correct pronunciation.

12. True. People want to know this.

13. False. Business is gender-neutral. However, there are cultural differences.

14. False. Your clothing adds or detracts from your professional appearance.

15. During a meal, place the napkin on your chair when you excuse yourself.

16. True. This keeps your right hand free for shaking hands.

17. True. No doubt about this.

18. False. The writing on the business card would be too small to read.

19. If your mother told you to avoid discussing religion and politics, she was right.

20. False. Your clothing will reek of smoke, and this is a definite turnoff for most people.

Index

Technological Competency as Caring in Nursing, Locsin, 2005.

Making a Difference: Stories from the Point of Care, Volume 1, Hudacek, 2005.

A Daybook for Nurses: Making a Difference Each Day, Hudacek, 2004.

Making a Difference: Stories from the Point of Care, Volume 2, Hudacek, 2004.

Building and Managing a Career in Nursing: Strategies for Advancing Your Career, Miller, 2003.

Collaboration for the Promotion of Nursing, Briggs, Merk, and Mitchell, 2003.

Ordinary People, Extraordinary Lives: The Stories of Nurses, Smeltzer and Vlasses, 2003.

Stories of Family Caregiving: Reconsideration of Theory, Literature, and Life, Poirier and Ayres, 2002.

As We See Ourselves: Jewish Women in Nursing, Benson, 2001.

Cadet Nurse Stories: The Call for and Response of Women During World War II, Perry and Robinson, 2001.

Creating Responsive Solutions to Healthcare Change, McCullough, 2001.

The Language of Nursing Theory and Metatheory, King and Fawcett, 1997.

For more information and to order these books from the Honor Society of Nursing, Sigma Theta Tau International, visit the honor society's Web site at www.nursingsociety.org/publications, or go to www.nursingknowledge.org/stti/books, the Web site of Nursing Knowledge International, the honor society's sales and distribution division. Or, call 1.888.NKI.4.YOU (U.S. and Canada) or +1.317.634.8171 (Outside U.S. and Canada).